The BIG, FUN KIDS BAKING BOOK

kids
HEARST
HOME

## Food Network Magazine

**Editor in Chief** Maile Carpenter
**Creative Director** Deirdre Koribanick
**Executive Editor** Liz Sgroi
**Managing Editor** Robb Riedel
**Photo Director** Alice Albert
**Special Projects Editor** Pamela Mitchell

### FEATURES
**Deputy Editor** Jessica Dodell-Feder
**Food Editor** Ariana Phillips Tessier
**Contributing Food Editor** Teri Tsang Barrett
**Associate Editors** Kate Trombly O'Brien, Kara Zauberman
**Assistant Editor** Cory Fernandez

### ART AND PHOTOGRAPHY
**Art Director** Rachel Keaveny
**Deputy Art Director** Amy Kaffka
**Associate Photo Editor** Amy McNulty
**Assistant Photo Editor** Mollie Kingsbury
**Digital Imaging Specialist** Ruth Vázquez

### COPY
**Copy Chief** Chris Jagger
**Research Chief** Katherine Wessling
**Copy Editors** David Cobb Craig, Ian Hodder,
Clare O'Shea, Joy Sanchez

### FOOD NETWORK KITCHEN
**Test Kitchen Director** Stephen Jackson
**Recipe Developers** Melissa Gaman, Young Sun Huh,
Khalil Hymore, Amy Stevenson
**Recipe Tester** Jessica Widmer

### HEARST HOME KIDS
**Vice President & Publisher** Jacqueline Deval
**Editor** Nicole Fisher
**Marketing Coordinator** Nickolas Young

### HEARST MAGAZINE MEDIA, INC.
**President & Treasurer** Debi Chirichella
**Chief Content Officer** Kate Lewis
**Chief Business Officer** Kristen M. O'Hara
**Secretary** Catherine A. Bostron

**Publishing Consultants** Gilbert C. Maurer, Mark F. Miller

### HEARST
**President & Chief Executive Officer** Steven R. Swartz
**Chairman** William R. Hearst III
**Executive Vice Chairman** Frank A. Bennack, Jr.

Book design by Rachel Keaveny.

Illustrations by Amy Kaffka.

Library of Congress Cataloging-in-Publication Data is available.

10  9  8  7  6  5  4  3  2  1

Published by Hearst Home Kids, an imprint of
Hearst Books/Hearst Magazine Media, Inc.
300 West 57th Street
New York, NY 10019

Printed in China.

ISBN 978-1-950785-30-8

To all the future
pastry chefs:
Keep calm and bake on!

**Question: Are you a cook or are you a baker?**
Before you answer that, let's put it another way: When you're in the kitchen, do you like to throw a little of this and a handful of that into the pan and see what happens? Or do you like to take your time, measure everything carefully and follow recipes just as they're written? If the second description sounds more like you, then congratulations—you're a baker! And you're in the right place, because this book is full of recipes for bakers at every level, whether you're just starting out or you're already a cookie-making, cake-leveling, cupcake-decorating whiz.

We bake like crazy in Food Network Kitchen, and not just because we love a homemade treat. Baking makes us *happy*. We love everything about it: choosing what to make, lining up the ingredients, picking out the perfect sprinkles. We love the anticipation, too, as we wait oh-so-patiently for things to bake and cool. If you flip through these pages you'll see some pretty spectacular desserts, and we promise that every single one of them is doable. It's true. You—the baker in the house—can tackle anything you see in here, so we just have one more question: What will you make first?

Maile Carpenter
Editor in Chief

Liz Sgroi
Executive Editor

# CONTENTS

# Muffins & Quick Breads

**16**
Salted Caramel
Chocolate Muffins

**17**
Carrot-Coconut
Muffins

**18**
Apple-Pumpkin
Muffins

**19**
Cherry-Pistachio
Muffins

**20**
Lemon-Poppy Seed
Zucchini Muffins

**21**
Blueberry-Nectarine
Muffins

**23**
Apple-Cranberry
Muffins

**24**
Snickerdoodle
Muffins

**25**
Caramel-Pumpkin
Muffins

**27**
Strawberry
Corn Muffins

**29**
Design-Your-Own
Banana Bread

**30**
Blueberry-Corn
Quick Bread

**31**
Chocolate-Peanut Butter
Chip Quick Bread

**32**
Carrot-Raisin
Quick Bread

**34**
Lemon-Raspberry
Quick Bread

**35**
Blueberry-Almond
Quick Bread

# Brownies & Bars

**40**
Classic
Brownies

**41**
Chocolate-
Hazelnut Brownies

**43**
Red Velvet Brownies

**44**
Mint
Brownies

**45**
Chocolate-Frosted
Brownies

**46**
Peanut Butter
Cup Brownies

**47**
Butterscotch
Blondies

**50**
Snickerdoodle
Bars

**51**
Trail Mix Bars

**52**
Triple-Decker
Bars

**53**
Butterscotch
Pretzel Bars

**54**
Chocolate-
Pecan Bars

**56**
Birthday Cake
Bars

**57**
Chocolate Chip
Cookie Bars

**58**
Sweet-and-Salty
Snack Bars

**59**
Gluten-Free
Peanut Butter Bars

**61**
Chunky Monkey Bars

**62**
Sugar Cookie
Bars

**63**
Confetti
Magic Bars

**64**
Oatmeal-Raisin
Cookie Bars

**65**
Lemon Bars

# Cookies

70
Red Velvet-White Chocolate Chip Cookies

71
Snack Attack Cookies with Bacon

72
Pumpkin Spice Chocolate Chip Cookies

73
Loaded Chocolate Cookies

74
Triple Chocolate-Hazelnut Cookies

76
Confetti Biscotti

77
S'mores Chocolate Chip Cookies

78
Chocolate-Raspberry Cookies

79
Chocolate-Mint Chip Cookies

80
Chewy Ginger Cookies

81
PB Oatmeal-Chocolate Chip Cookies

82
Sugar Cookies with Royal Icing

83
PB&J Sandwich Cookies

85
Design-Your-Own Whoopie Pies

87
Plum Pie Cookies

88
Red Velvet Crackle Cookies

89
Lime Crackle Cookies

90
Rainbow Cookies

92
Gluten-Free Coconut Snowballs

93
Milk Chocolate Cookie Cups

95
Lemonade Pinwheels

# Cupcakes

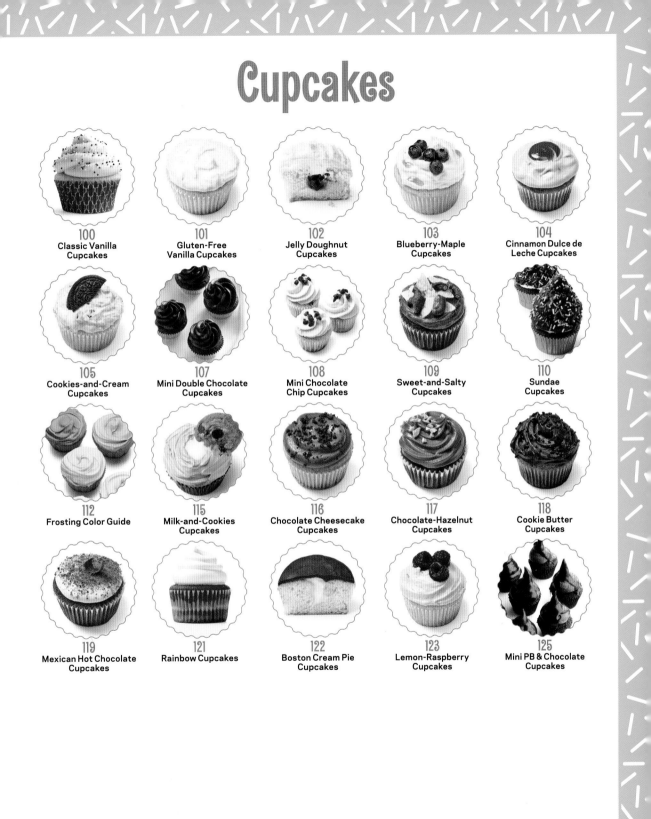

**100**
Classic Vanilla
Cupcakes

**101**
Gluten-Free
Vanilla Cupcakes

**102**
Jelly Doughnut
Cupcakes

**103**
Blueberry-Maple
Cupcakes

**104**
Cinnamon Dulce de
Leche Cupcakes

**105**
Cookies-and-Cream
Cupcakes

**107**
Mini Double Chocolate
Cupcakes

**108**
Mini Chocolate
Chip Cupcakes

**109**
Sweet-and-Salty
Cupcakes

**110**
Sundae
Cupcakes

**112**
Frosting Color Guide

**115**
Milk-and-Cookies
Cupcakes

**116**
Chocolate Cheesecake
Cupcakes

**117**
Chocolate-Hazelnut
Cupcakes

**118**
Cookie Butter
Cupcakes

**119**
Mexican Hot Chocolate
Cupcakes

**121**
Rainbow Cupcakes

**122**
Boston Cream Pie
Cupcakes

**123**
Lemon-Raspberry
Cupcakes

**125**
Mini PB & Chocolate
Cupcakes

# Cakes

**131**
Chocolate Candy Bar
Layer Cake

**132**
Basic Vanilla Cake

**133**
Cookies-and-Cream
Cake

**135**
Strawberry Shortcake
Layer Cake

**136**
Triple Chocolate Cake

**139**
S'mores Cake

**141**
Design-Your-Own
Rainbow Layer Cake

**142**
Red Velvet
Layer Cake

**143**
Root Beer
Bundt Cake

**145**
Peanut Tunnel of
Fudge Cake

**146**
Mint Chip
Sheet Cake

**147**
Lemon
Sheet Cake

**148**
PB&J
Sheet Cake

**149**
Rainbow Sheet Cake

**150**
Tres Leches Cake
with Mango

**153**
Chocolate-Zucchini
Cake

# Fake-Out Cakes

**158**
Ants-on-a-Log
Cakes

**160**
Egg-in-a-Hole
Cake

**162**
Chili Dog Cake

**164**
Pineapple Cake

**166**
Spaghetti-and-Meatballs
Cake

**168**
Maki Cake

**170**
Pencil Cake

**172**
Taco Ice Cream
Cake

**174**
Ice Cream Sandwich
Cake

**176**
Grilled Cheese
Cake

**178**
Caramel
Apple Cake

# Just for Fun

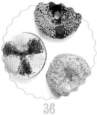

**36**
Decorated
Doughnuts

**66**
Blondie Jenga

**97**
Cookie Puzzle

**126**
Candy Melt
Cupcake Toppers

**154**
DIY Sprinkles

# muffins & quick breads

# Salted Caramel Chocolate Muffins

ACTIVE: **30 min**    TOTAL: **1 hr (plus cooling)**    MAKES: **12**

1½  cups all-purpose flour

¾  cup sugar

½  cup unsweetened cocoa powder

2  teaspoons baking powder

¼  teaspoon baking soda

¼  teaspoon salt

⅓  cup chopped semisweet chocolate, plus more chocolate for grating

1  cup whole milk

½  cup vegetable oil

2  large eggs

½  cup jarred dulce de leche (it should be thick)

Flaky salt, for topping

1  Preheat the oven to 375°F. Line a 12-cup muffin pan with paper liners. Mix the flour, sugar, cocoa powder, baking powder, baking soda and salt in a large bowl with a whisk. Add the chopped chocolate and whisk until combined. In a small bowl, whisk the milk, vegetable oil and eggs until smooth. Add the milk mixture to the flour mixture and stir with a rubber spatula until just combined.

2  Spoon the batter evenly into the muffin cups, filling them about two-thirds of the way. Bake until the edges of the muffins are just set but the centers are still loose, 8 to 10 minutes. Remove the pan from the oven with oven mitts. Working quickly, spoon 1 heaping teaspoon dulce de leche into the center of each muffin. Return the pan to the oven and bake until the batter rises over the dulce de leche and a toothpick inserted into a muffin (but not into the dulce de leche) comes out clean, 10 to 15 minutes. Remove the pan from the oven with oven mitts.

3  Using a grater or zester, grate more chocolate over the tops of the hot muffins and sprinkle with flaky salt. Let the muffins cool 5 minutes in the pan, then remove from the pan and let cool completely on a rack.

# Carrot-Coconut Muffins

ACTIVE: **30 min**   TOTAL: **1 hr (plus cooling)**   MAKES: **12**

## FOR THE MUFFINS

1½ cups all-purpose flour

1   teaspoon ground cinnamon

1   teaspoon baking powder

¼   teaspoon baking soda

½   teaspoon ground ginger

½   teaspoon salt

¾   cup packed light brown sugar

½   cup plain whole-milk yogurt

⅓   cup coconut oil, melted

2   large eggs

1   teaspoon pure vanilla extract

1½ cups grated carrots
    (about 3 carrots)

½   cup sweetened shredded
    coconut

½   cup chopped macadamia nuts

¼   cup finely chopped
    crystallized ginger

## FOR THE GLAZE

½   cup confectioners' sugar

2   teaspoons water

Sweetened shredded coconut, for
    topping

**1** Make the muffins: Preheat the oven to 375°F. Line a 12-cup muffin pan with paper liners. Mix the flour, cinnamon, baking powder, baking soda, ground ginger and salt in a large bowl with a whisk; make a well in the center. In a small bowl, whisk the brown sugar, yogurt, melted coconut oil, eggs and vanilla. Pour the yogurt mixture into the well in the flour mixture and stir with a rubber spatula until combined. Add the carrots, coconut, nuts and crystallized ginger and fold together with the rubber spatula.

**2** Spoon the batter evenly into the muffin cups, filling them about three-quarters of the way. Bake until the muffins are golden and a toothpick inserted into the center of a muffin comes out clean, 20 to 25 minutes. Remove the pan from the oven with oven mitts. Let the muffins cool 5 minutes in the pan, then remove from the pan and let cool completely on a rack.

**3** Meanwhile, make the glaze: Stir the confectioners' sugar with the water in a small bowl. Spread about 1 teaspoon glaze on each muffin and top with coconut.

# Apple-Pumpkin Muffins

ACTIVE: **45 min**    TOTAL: **1 hr 15 min (plus cooling)**    MAKES: **12**

## FOR THE MUFFINS

- **1**   Granny Smith apple
- **½**   cup plus 1 teaspoon granulated sugar
- **7**   tablespoons unsalted butter, melted
- **1**   teaspoon plus a pinch of ground cinnamon
- **½**   teaspoon plus a pinch of salt
- **2**   cups all-purpose flour
- **1**   tablespoon baking powder
- **1**   cup whole milk
- **½**   cup canned pure pumpkin puree
- **1**   teaspoon pure vanilla extract
- **2**   large eggs

## FOR THE GLAZE

- **½**   cup confectioners' sugar
- **1½ to 2½**   teaspoons whole milk
- **¼**   teaspoon pure vanilla extract

**1** Make the muffins: Preheat the oven to 350°F. Line a 12-cup muffin pan with paper liners. Peel the apple, cut into 12 wedges, then slice the wedges crosswise into small triangular pieces. Combine the apple pieces, 1 teaspoon granulated sugar, 1 tablespoon melted butter and a pinch each of cinnamon and salt in a large nonstick skillet. Cook over medium-high heat, stirring occasionally, until the apples are browned, 4 to 6 minutes. Let cool completely.

**2** Mix the flour, baking powder and the remaining 1 teaspoon cinnamon and ½ teaspoon salt in a large bowl with a whisk. In a medium bowl, whisk the remaining ½ cup granulated sugar and 6 tablespoons melted butter, the milk, pumpkin puree, vanilla and eggs. Add the pumpkin mixture to the flour mixture and stir with a rubber spatula until just combined.

**3** Spoon the batter evenly into the muffin cups, filling them about three-quarters of the way. Spoon the apples into the center of each. Bake until a toothpick inserted into the center of a muffin comes out clean, 22 to 25 minutes. Remove the pan from the oven with oven mitts. Let the muffins cool 5 minutes in the pan, then remove from the pan and let cool completely on a rack.

**4** Meanwhile, make the glaze: Stir the confectioners' sugar with 1½ teaspoons milk and the vanilla in a small bowl until smooth, gradually adding 1 more teaspoon milk if needed. Drizzle the glaze over the muffins. Let set 10 minutes.

## Did You Know?

A pumpkin is a fruit, not a vegetable. All squashes are technically fruits because they develop from flowers and contain seeds.

# Cherry-Pistachio Muffins

ACTIVE: **30 min**    TOTAL: **1 hr (plus cooling)**    MAKES: **12**

½    **cup pistachios**

⅓    **cup all-purpose flour**

1    **teaspoon baking powder**

¼    **teaspoon salt**

⅔    **cup confectioners' sugar, plus more for topping**

2    **large eggs**

6    **tablespoons unsalted butter, melted**

**12 to 24 medium fresh cherries with stems**

### Tip

We love the way these cherries look, but you can't bite into them whole—they still have pits! Just pull them off and eat them separately.

**1** Preheat the oven to 350°F. Line a 12-cup muffin pan with paper liners. Combine the pistachios, flour, baking powder and salt in a food processor and pulse until finely ground.

**2** Mix the confectioners' sugar and eggs in a large bowl with a whisk. Add the pistachio mixture and whisk until just combined. Add the melted butter and stir with a rubber spatula until just combined.

**3** Spoon the batter evenly into the muffin cups. Bake until the muffins are slightly puffed and just beginning to set, about 8 minutes. Remove the pan from the oven with oven mitts. Place 1 or 2 cherries in the center of each muffin. Return to the oven and bake until the muffins feel springy and the edges are lightly browned, 10 to 12 minutes. Remove from the oven. Let the muffins cool 10 minutes in the pan, then remove the pan and let cool completely on a rack. Sprinkle with confectioners' sugar.

# Lemon-Poppy Seed Zucchini Muffins

ACTIVE: **30 min**    TOTAL: **1 hr (plus cooling)**    MAKES: **12**

1    **lemon**

1    **cup sugar**

2    **teaspoons poppy seeds**

1½    **cups all-purpose flour**

½    **teaspoon baking soda**

½    **teaspoon baking powder**

½    **teaspoon salt**

½    **cup vegetable oil**

¼    **cup buttermilk or plain yogurt (not Greek)**

½    **teaspoon pure vanilla extract**

2    **large eggs**

1    **cup packed grated zucchini (about 1 zucchini)**

**1** Preheat the oven to 350°F. Line a 12-cup muffin pan with paper liners. Using a vegetable peeler, remove the zest from the lemon in wide strips, being careful not to remove the white part (called the pith). Put the lemon zest and sugar in a food processor and process until the zest is finely chopped, scraping the sides of the food processor with a rubber spatula. Scrape the lemon sugar into a small bowl and stir in the poppy seeds.

**2** Mix the flour, baking soda, baking powder and salt in a large bowl with a whisk. In a medium bowl, whisk the vegetable oil, buttermilk, vanilla and eggs. Set aside 3 tablespoons of the lemon–poppy seed sugar, then add the rest of the lemon–poppy seed sugar to the bowl with the buttermilk mixture. Add the buttermilk mixture to the flour mixture and stir with a rubber spatula until just combined. Stir in the grated zucchini.

**3** Spoon the batter evenly into the muffin cups, filling them about three-quarters of the way. Tap the bottom of the pan lightly against the counter to smooth out the batter. Sprinkle the tops of the muffins with the remaining 3 tablespoons lemon–poppy seed sugar. Bake until a toothpick inserted into the center of a muffin comes out clean, 23 to 25 minutes. Remove the pan from the oven with oven mitts. Let the muffins cool 5 minutes in the pan, then remove from the pan and let cool completely on a rack.

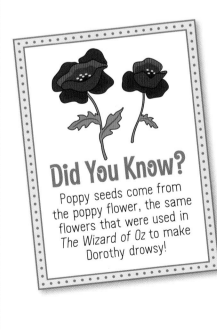

## Did You Know?

Poppy seeds come from the poppy flower, the same flowers that were used in *The Wizard of Oz* to make Dorothy drowsy!

# Blueberry-Nectarine Muffins

ACTIVE: 30 min    TOTAL: 50 min (plus cooling)    MAKES: 12

2    cups all-purpose flour
½    teaspoon baking powder
½    teaspoon baking soda
½    teaspoon salt
⅔    cup granulated sugar
½    cup vegetable oil
½    cup sour cream
2    large eggs
¼    teaspoon pure almond extract
2    small nectarines, pitted and chopped (about 1¾ cups)
½    cup blueberries
¼    cup sliced almonds
Coarse sugar, for topping

1  Preheat the oven to 400°F. Line a 12-cup muffin pan with paper liners. Mix the flour, baking powder, baking soda and salt in a large bowl with a whisk. In a medium bowl, whisk the granulated sugar, vegetable oil, sour cream, eggs and almond extract. Add the sour cream mixture to the flour mixture and stir with a rubber spatula until just combined. Stir in the nectarines and blueberries.

2  Spoon the batter evenly into the muffin cups, filling them about three-quarters of the way. Sprinkle the almonds on top, then sprinkle with coarse sugar. Bake until the muffins are golden and the tops spring back when gently pressed, about 20 minutes. Remove the pan from the oven with oven mitts. Let the muffins cool 5 minutes in the pan, then remove from the pan and let cool completely on a rack.

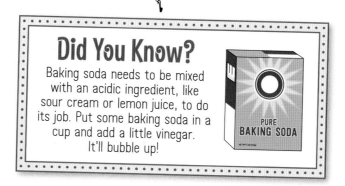

## Did You Know?

Baking soda needs to be mixed with an acidic ingredient, like sour cream or lemon juice, to do its job. Put some baking soda in a cup and add a little vinegar. It'll bubble up!

PURE BAKING SODA

# Apple-Cranberry Muffins

ACTIVE: **30 min**   TOTAL: **1 hr (plus cooling)**   MAKES: **12**

Cooking spray

2   cups all-purpose flour

½   cup dried cranberries,
    plus more for topping

1   teaspoon baking powder

½   teaspoon salt

½   teaspoon ground cinnamon

¼   teaspoon baking soda

¾   cup packed light
    brown sugar

1   stick unsalted butter,
    melted

½   cup applesauce

½   cup sour cream

2   large eggs

Dried apple slices, for topping

**1** Preheat the oven to 350°F. Line a 12-cup muffin pan with paper or foil liners. Lightly coat the liners with cooking spray. Mix the flour, dried cranberries, baking powder, salt, cinnamon and baking soda in a large bowl with a whisk. In a medium bowl, whisk the brown sugar, melted butter, applesauce, sour cream and eggs. Add the applesauce mixture to the flour mixture and stir with a rubber spatula until combined.

**2** Spoon the batter evenly into the muffin cups, filling them about two-thirds to three-quarters of the way. Top each with a few dried apple slices and more dried cranberries. Bake until a toothpick inserted into the center of a muffin comes out clean, 20 to 25 minutes. Remove the pan from the oven with oven mitts. Let the muffins cool 5 minutes in the pan, then remove from the pan and let cool completely on a rack.

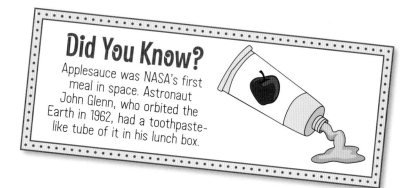

## Did You Know?

Applesauce was NASA's first meal in space. Astronaut John Glenn, who orbited the Earth in 1962, had a toothpaste-like tube of it in his lunch box.

# Snickerdoodle Muffins

ACTIVE: **30 min**    TOTAL: **1 hr (plus cooling)**    MAKES: **12**

Cooking spray

¾  cup plus ⅔ cup sugar

2⅓ cups all-purpose flour

1   tablespoon plus ½ teaspoon
    ground cinnamon

1½ sticks (12 tablespoons) unsalted
    butter, at room temperature

1   teaspoon baking powder

½   teaspoon salt

¼   teaspoon baking soda

3   large eggs

1   cup sour cream

1   teaspoon pure vanilla extract

1 Preheat the oven to 350°F. Line a 12-cup muffin pan with paper or foil liners. Coat the liners with cooking spray. Make the crumble: Mix ⅔ cup sugar, ⅓ cup flour and 1 tablespoon cinnamon in a small bowl with a whisk. Add ½ stick butter and mash with a spoon. Set the crumble aside. Put the remaining 1 stick butter in a microwave-safe bowl and melt in the microwave.

2 Mix the remaining 2 cups flour and ½ teaspoon cinnamon, the baking powder, salt and baking soda in a large bowl with a whisk. In a medium bowl, whisk the eggs, remaining ¾ cup sugar, the melted butter, sour cream and vanilla. Add the egg mixture to the flour mixture and stir with a rubber spatula. Stir ½ cup of the crumble mixture into the batter.

3 Spoon the batter evenly into the muffin cups, filling them about two-thirds of the way. Top with the remaining crumble. Bake until a toothpick inserted into the center of a muffin comes out clean, 25 to 28 minutes. Remove the pan from the oven with oven mitts. Let the muffins cool 5 minutes in the pan, then remove from the pan and let cool completely on a rack.

# Caramel-Pumpkin Muffins

ACTIVE: 30 min   TOTAL: 1 hr (plus cooling)   MAKES: 12

- **2** cups all-purpose flour
- **½** cup granulated sugar
- **½** cup chopped pecans, toasted (see tip)
- **1** teaspoon baking powder
- **½** teaspoon salt
- **¼** teaspoon baking soda
- **2** large eggs
- **½** cup jarred caramel sauce, plus more for brushing
- **½** cup canned pure pumpkin puree
- **½** cup sour cream
- **1** stick unsalted butter, melted
- **¼** cup packed light brown sugar

1. Preheat the oven to 350°F. Line a 12-cup muffin pan with paper liners. Mix the flour, granulated sugar, pecans, baking powder, salt and baking soda in a large bowl with a whisk. In a medium bowl, whisk the eggs, caramel sauce, pumpkin puree, sour cream, melted butter and brown sugar. Add the caramel mixture to the flour mixture and stir with a rubber spatula.

2. Spoon the batter evenly into the muffin cups. Bake until the muffins are golden, about 30 minutes. Remove the pan from the oven with oven mitts. While the muffins are still warm, top them with more caramel sauce using a pastry brush. Let the muffins cool 5 minutes in the pan, then remove from the pan and let cool completely on a rack.

## Tip

If you're baking with nuts, toast them first to bring out the flavor. Spread on a baking sheet and bake at 350°F for 8 to 12 minutes, stirring halfway through.

Try whipping the cream by hand: It's a serious workout! Whisk it in a chilled bowl until soft peaks form—it'll take a few minutes.

# Strawberry Corn Muffins

ACTIVE: **30 min**   TOTAL: **45 min (plus cooling)**   MAKES: **6**

Cooking spray

1   **8.5-ounce package corn muffin mix (plus required ingredients)**

¼   **cup all-purpose flour**

2   **teaspoons grated lemon zest**

1   **teaspoon pure vanilla extract**

1   **cup chopped fresh strawberries**

2   **tablespoons strawberry preserves**

¾   **cup heavy cream**

2   **tablespoons confectioners' sugar**

**1** Preheat the oven to 375°F. Lightly coat a 6-cup muffin pan with cooking spray. Prepare the corn muffin mix as the label directs. Stir in the flour, lemon zest and vanilla with a rubber spatula.

**2** Spoon the batter evenly into the muffin cups. Bake until the edges of the muffins are set and the centers are soft but not wet, 10 to 12 minutes. Meanwhile, toss the strawberries and strawberry preserves in a bowl.

**3** Remove the pan from the oven with oven mitts. Gently press the back of a teaspoon into the center of each muffin to make an indentation about one-third of the way into the muffins. Spoon 2 teaspoons of the strawberry mixture into each indentation, pressing to tightly fill. (Save the rest of the strawberry mixture for topping.) Return the pan to the oven and continue baking until the muffins are golden, about 5 more minutes. Remove the pan from the oven. Let the muffins cool 5 minutes in the pan, then remove from the pan and let cool completely on a rack.

**4** Beat the heavy cream and confectioners' sugar in a large bowl with a mixer until soft peaks form. Top the muffins with the remaining berry mixture and serve with the whipped cream.

### Did You Know?
Jiffy corn muffin mix, which debuted in 1950, is one of the best-selling dry grocery products in the US!

DESIGN YOUR OWN RECIPE

# Banana Bread

Chocolate Chip
Banana Bread
with Chocolate
Glaze

## 1

## Pick Your Mix-Ins

Choose one or two mix-ins and measure out 1¾ cups total (don't use more than ¾ cup nuts).
Chop any nuts or any large pieces of dried fruit.

**Nuts**
(such as walnuts,
pecans or almonds)

**Dried fruit**
(such as apricots or
cranberries)

**Chocolate
chips**

**Rolled
oats**

**Sweetened
shredded coconut**

## 2

## Make the Batter

- Preheat the oven to 350°F and butter a 9-by-5-inch loaf pan. Mix 1¼ cups flour, ¾ cup granulated sugar, 1 teaspoon each baking powder and salt, and ½ teaspoon each baking soda and cinnamon in a large bowl with a whisk. Stir in your mix-ins (from step 1).

- In a medium bowl, whisk 2 eggs, ½ cup cooled melted butter or vegetable oil, ½ cup plain yogurt or sour cream and 1 teaspoon vanilla.

- Add 1 cup mashed banana to the egg mixture and whisk until combined, then add to the flour mixture and stir with a rubber spatula.

## 3

## Bake the Loaf

Spread the batter in the loaf pan. Bake until a toothpick inserted into the center of the loaf comes out clean, about 55 minutes. Remove the pan with oven mitts, place on a rack and let the bread cool 30 minutes in the pan. Remove the loaf from the pan and let it cool completely on the rack.

## 4

## Make a Glaze

Prepare a glaze, pour on the cooled bread and let set 15 to 20 minutes.

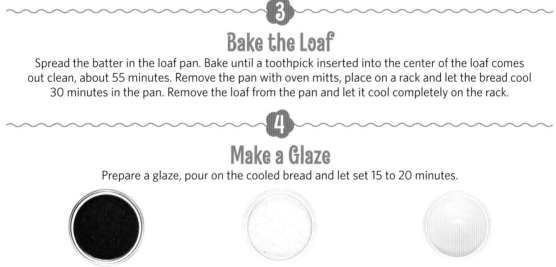

**CHOCOLATE**
Whisk 1 cup confectioners' sugar,
2 tablespoons cocoa powder,
2 tablespoons milk, ¼ teaspoon
vanilla and a pinch of salt.

**VANILLA**
Whisk 1 cup confectioners'
sugar, 1 tablespoon milk
and the seeds from
1 vanilla bean.

**CREAM CHEESE**
Mix 1 cup confectioners' sugar,
3 tablespoons softened cream
cheese, 2 tablespoons milk and
¼ teaspoon vanilla.

# Blueberry-Corn Quick Bread

ACTIVE: **25 min**    TOTAL: **1½ hr (plus cooling)**    MAKES: **one 9-inch loaf**

Cooking spray

1¼ cups all-purpose flour, plus 1 tablespoon for the blueberries

½ cup fine yellow cornmeal

1¼ teaspoons baking powder

½ teaspoon salt

1 stick unsalted butter, at room temperature

¾ cup sugar

2 large eggs

1½ teaspoons pure vanilla extract

¾ cup whole milk

Grated zest of 1 lemon

1¼ cups blueberries

**1** Preheat the oven to 350°F. Line a 9-by-5-inch loaf pan with parchment paper, leaving an overhang on two sides. Coat the paper well with cooking spray.

**2** Mix 1¼ cups flour, the cornmeal, baking powder and salt in a medium bowl with a whisk. In a large bowl, beat the butter and sugar with a mixer on medium speed until fluffy. Beat the eggs and vanilla into the butter mixture until combined, then beat in the milk and lemon zest. Add the flour mixture and beat until combined.

**3** Using your fingers, toss the blueberries with the remaining 1 tablespoon flour in a medium bowl. Add the blueberries to the batter and gently stir with a rubber spatula.

**4** Scrape the batter into the loaf pan. Bake until a toothpick inserted into the center of the bread comes out clean, 55 to 65 minutes. Remove the pan from the oven with oven mitts, place on a rack and let the bread cool 1 hour in the pan. Then use the overhanging parchment to lift the loaf out of the pan and let it cool completely on the rack.

## Tip

Toss mix-ins like fresh berries, chocolate chips or dried fruit with flour before you add them to a batter. This will keep them from sinking to the bottom!

# Chocolate-Peanut Butter Chip Quick Bread

ACTIVE: **25 min**    TOTAL: **1 hr 35 min (plus cooling)**    MAKES: **one 9-inch loaf**

Cooking spray

1½ **cups sour cream**

½ **cup vegetable oil**

2 **large eggs**

1 **teaspoon pure vanilla extract**

1½ **cups all-purpose flour**

¾ **cup sugar**

¼ **cup unsweetened cocoa powder**

1 **teaspoon baking powder**

½ **teaspoon salt**

¼ **teaspoon baking soda**

¾ **cup peanut butter chips**

¼ **cup semisweet chocolate chips**

½ **cup chopped salted peanuts**

**1** Preheat the oven to 350°F. Line a 9-by-5-inch loaf pan with parchment paper, leaving an overhang on two sides. Coat the paper with cooking spray.

**2** Mix the sour cream, vegetable oil, eggs and vanilla in a medium bowl with a whisk. In a large bowl, whisk the flour, sugar, cocoa powder, baking powder, salt and baking soda. Stir in the peanut butter chips and chocolate chips. Add the sour cream mixture to the flour mixture and mix with a rubber spatula until combined.

**3** Scrape the batter into the loaf pan. Sprinkle the peanuts down the center of the batter. Bake until a toothpick inserted into the center of the bread comes out clean, 60 to 70 minutes. Remove the pan from the oven with oven mitts, place on a rack and let the bread cool 1 hour in the pan. Then use the overhanging parchment to lift the loaf out of the pan and let it cool completely on the rack.

# Carrot-Raisin Quick Bread

ACTIVE: **30 min**    TOTAL: **1 hr 35 min (plus cooling)**    MAKES: **one 9-inch loaf**

## FOR THE BREAD

Cooking spray

2   carrots, shredded (1 cup)

½   cup vegetable oil

½   cup plain yogurt

2   large eggs

1   teaspoon pure
    vanilla extract

1½  cups all-purpose flour

¾   cup granulated sugar

½   cup sweetened shredded
    coconut

½   cup golden raisins

1   teaspoon baking powder

1   teaspoon ground cinnamon

½   teaspoon salt

¼   teaspoon baking soda

¼   teaspoon ground nutmeg

## FOR THE GLAZE

2   ounces cream cheese,
    at room temperature

3   tablespoons whole milk

2   tablespoons confectioners'
    sugar

Pinch of salt

**1** Make the bread: Preheat the oven to 350°F. Line a 9-by-5-inch loaf pan with parchment paper, leaving an overhang on two sides. Coat the paper well with cooking spray.

**2** Mix the carrots, vegetable oil, yogurt, eggs and vanilla in a medium bowl with a whisk. In a large bowl, whisk the flour, granulated sugar, coconut, raisins, baking powder, cinnamon, salt, baking soda and nutmeg. Add the carrot mixture to the flour mixture and stir with a rubber spatula until combined.

**3** Scrape the batter into the loaf pan. Bake until a toothpick inserted into the center of the bread comes out clean, 55 to 65 minutes. Remove the pan from the oven with oven mitts, place on a rack and let the bread cool 1 hour in the pan. Then use the overhanging parchment paper to lift the loaf out of the pan onto the rack.

**4** Make the glaze: Mix the cream cheese, milk, confectioners' sugar and salt in a small bowl. Drizzle over the warm bread and let cool completely.

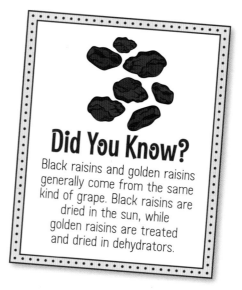

## Did You Know?
Black raisins and golden raisins generally come from the same kind of grape. Black raisins are dried in the sun, while golden raisins are treated and dried in dehydrators.

## Tip

Shred the carrots for this loaf on the large holes of a box grater. Don't use bagged preshredded carrots—they're too thick for baking.

# Lemon-Raspberry Quick Bread

ACTIVE: **25 min**    TOTAL: **1½ hr (plus cooling)**    MAKES: **one 9-inch loaf**

Cooking spray

1¾ cups **all-purpose flour**

1¼ teaspoons **baking powder**

½ teaspoon **salt**

1 stick **unsalted butter, at room temperature**

¾ cup **sugar**

2 large **eggs**

1½ teaspoons **pure vanilla extract**

¾ cup **whole milk**

Grated zest of **1 lemon**

⅓ cup **raspberry jam, warmed**

**1** Preheat the oven to 350°F. Line a 9-by-5-inch loaf pan with parchment paper, leaving an overhang on two sides. Coat the paper well with cooking spray.

**2** Mix the flour, baking powder and salt in a medium bowl with a whisk. In a large bowl, beat the butter and sugar with a mixer on medium speed until fluffy. Beat the eggs and vanilla into the butter mixture until combined, then beat in the milk and lemon zest. Add the flour mixture to the butter mixture and beat until combined.

**3** Scrape the batter into the loaf pan. Pour the raspberry jam over the batter and swirl with a butter knife. Bake until a toothpick inserted into the center of the bread comes out clean, 55 to 65 minutes. Remove the pan from the oven with oven mitts, place on a rack and let the bread cool 1 hour in the pan. Then use the overhanging parchment paper to lift the loaf out of the pan and let it cool completely on the rack.

## Did You Know?

The white part right under the peel on a lemon or other citrus fruit is called the pith. It's super bitter, so try to avoid it when you grate the zest.

# Blueberry-Almond Quick Bread

ACTIVE: **25 min**    TOTAL: **1½ hr (plus cooling)**    MAKES: **one 9-inch loaf**

Cooking spray
½  cup vegetable oil
½  cup plain yogurt
2  large eggs
1  teaspoon pure
   vanilla extract
1½ cups plus 1 tablespoon
   all-purpose flour
¾  cup sugar
½  cup sliced almonds
½  cup rolled oats
1  teaspoon baking powder
1  teaspoon ground cinnamon
½  teaspoon salt
¼  teaspoon baking soda
¼  teaspoon ground nutmeg
1¼ cups blueberries

1 Preheat the oven to 350°F. Line a 9-by-5-inch loaf pan with parchment paper, leaving an overhang on two sides. Coat the paper well with cooking spray.

2 Mix the vegetable oil, yogurt, eggs and vanilla in a medium bowl with a whisk. In a large bowl, whisk 1½ cups flour, the sugar, almonds, oats, baking powder, cinnamon, salt, baking soda and nutmeg. Add the yogurt mixture to the flour mixture and stir with a rubber spatula until combined.

3 Using your fingers, toss the blueberries with the remaining 1 tablespoon flour in a medium bowl. Add the blueberries to the batter and gently stir with the rubber spatula.

4 Scrape the batter into the loaf pan. Bake until a toothpick inserted into the center of the bread comes out clean, 55 to 65 minutes. Remove the pan from the oven with oven mitts, place on a rack and let the bread cool 1 hour in the pan. Then use the overhanging parchment paper to lift the loaf out of the pan and let it cool completely on the rack.

# Decorate Your Doughnuts

### How to Make the Glaze

Combine 2 cups confectioners' sugar with 2 to 3 tablespoons milk in a large bowl; mix with a whisk until smooth. Tint with food coloring. Dip plain cake doughnuts as directed for each design and let set.

### Sprinkle Stripes

Dip the top of a doughnut in the glaze. Sprinkle two different colors of sprinkles on each side.

### Sugar Pinwheel

Dip the top of a doughnut in the glaze. Sprinkle with two different colors of sanding sugar in a pinwheel pattern.

## Sweet Drizzle

Dip the top of a doughnut in the glaze. Let set. Drizzle with another color glaze.

## Super Spots

Dip the top of a doughnut in the glaze. Sprinkle with nonpareils.

## Golden Rings

Dip a doughnut in the glaze, making sure to get the sides and inside the hole. Sprinkle inside the hole with gold coarse sugar or sprinkles. Let set slightly, then roll the outside edge in more gold sugar.

# brownies & bars

**Tip**

Line the pan with foil and leave a little extra hanging over the sides so you can lift the brownies out of the pan after baking and cooling.

# Classic Brownies

ACTIVE: 20 min    TOTAL: 50 min (plus cooling)    MAKES: 24 to 30

Cooking spray

2   sticks unsalted butter

4   ounces semisweet chocolate, chopped

2   cups sugar

4   large eggs

1½  cups all-purpose flour

⅓   cup unsweetened cocoa powder

½   teaspoon salt

1  Preheat the oven to 350˚F. Line a 9-by-13-inch baking pan with foil, leaving a 2-inch overhang on two sides. Coat the foil with cooking spray. Combine the butter and chocolate in a large saucepan and cook over low heat, stirring with a rubber spatula, until melted. Remove from the heat and let cool slightly.

2  Add the sugar and eggs to the chocolate mixture and mix with a whisk until smooth. Add the flour, cocoa powder and salt and whisk until combined.

3  Spread the batter in the pan with the rubber spatula. Bake until a toothpick inserted into the center of the brownies comes out clean, 30 to 35 minutes. Remove the pan from the oven with oven mitts, put the pan on a rack and let the brownies cool completely.

4  Lift the brownies out of the pan using the overhanging foil, then peel off the foil. Cut the brownies into squares.

**Did You Know?**
In ancient Roman times, hazelnut plants were a popular gift—they were a symbol of happiness.

# Chocolate-Hazelnut Brownies

ACTIVE: 30 min    TOTAL: 1 hr (plus cooling)    MAKES: 24 to 30

## FOR THE BROWNIES
**Cooking spray**
- 2  **sticks unsalted butter**
- 4  **ounces semisweet chocolate, chopped**
- 2  **cups sugar**
- 4  **large eggs**
- 1½ **cups all-purpose flour**
- ⅓  **cup unsweetened cocoa powder**
- ½  **teaspoon salt**
- ¾  **cup chopped hazelnuts, plus more for topping**

## FOR THE FROSTING
- 1  **cup chocolate-hazelnut spread**
- 4  **tablespoons unsalted butter, at room temperature**
- 2  **tablespoons whole milk**

1. Make the brownies: Preheat the oven to 350˚F. Line a 9-by-13-inch baking pan with foil, leaving a 2-inch overhang on two sides. Coat the foil with cooking spray. Combine the butter and chocolate in a large saucepan and cook over low heat, stirring with a rubber spatula, until melted. Remove from the heat and let cool slightly.

2. Add the sugar and eggs to the chocolate mixture and mix with a whisk until smooth. Add the flour, cocoa powder and salt and whisk until combined. Stir in the hazelnuts with the rubber spatula.

3. Spread the batter in the pan with the rubber spatula. Bake until a toothpick inserted into the center of the brownies comes out clean, 30 to 35 minutes. Remove the pan from the oven with oven mitts, put the pan on a rack and let the brownies cool completely.

4. Meanwhile, make the frosting: Combine the chocolate-hazelnut spread, butter and milk in a medium bowl. Beat with a mixer on medium speed until smooth.

5. Lift the brownies out of the pan using the overhanging foil, then peel off the foil. Spread the frosting on top with an offset spatula or the back of a spoon. Top with hazelnuts. Cut the brownies into squares.

**Tip**

To avoid lumpy frosting, make sure your cream cheese and butter are at room temperature. Take them out of the fridge about an hour ahead.

# Red Velvet Brownies

ACTIVE: 30 min    TOTAL: 50 min (plus cooling)    MAKES: 24 to 30

## FOR THE BROWNIES

Cooking spray

1    cup all-purpose flour

3    tablespoons unsweetened cocoa powder

½    teaspoon salt

½    teaspoon baking powder

1½   cups packed dark brown sugar

1    stick unsalted butter

⅔    cup water

2    ounces unsweetened chocolate, chopped

3    large eggs

1½   teaspoons pure vanilla extract

2    teaspoons red liquid food coloring

## FOR THE FROSTING

8    ounces cream cheese, at room temperature

4    tablespoons unsalted butter, at room temperature

1½   cups confectioners' sugar

1    teaspoon pure vanilla extract

1. Make the brownies: Preheat the oven to 325°F. Line a 9-by-13-inch baking pan with foil, leaving a 2-inch overhang on two sides. Coat the foil with cooking spray. Mix the flour, cocoa powder, salt and baking powder in a small bowl with a whisk.

2. Combine the brown sugar, butter and water in a large saucepan. Bring to a simmer over medium heat, stirring with a whisk. Remove from the heat and whisk in the chocolate. Let cool slightly. Whisk in the eggs, one at a time, and then the vanilla and food coloring. Add the flour mixture and stir with a rubber spatula until combined.

3. Spread the batter in the pan using the rubber spatula. Bake until a toothpick inserted into the center of the brownies comes out almost clean, 20 to 25 minutes. Remove the pan from the oven with oven mitts, put the pan on a rack and let the brownies cool completely.

4. Meanwhile, make the frosting: Combine the cream cheese, butter, confectioners' sugar and vanilla in a large bowl. Beat with a mixer on medium speed until smooth.

5. Lift the brownies out of the pan using the overhanging foil, then peel off the foil. Spread the frosting on the brownies using an offset spatula or the back of a spoon. Cut the brownies into squares.

## Did You Know?
Most red velvet cakes these days call for food coloring, but the cakes originally got their color from raw cocoa powder, which turned reddish when mixed with the batter. Today's cakes are much brighter!

## Tip

Look for mint chocolate chips in the baking aisle—they might be brown or green—or just chop a mint chocolate bar into small pieces.

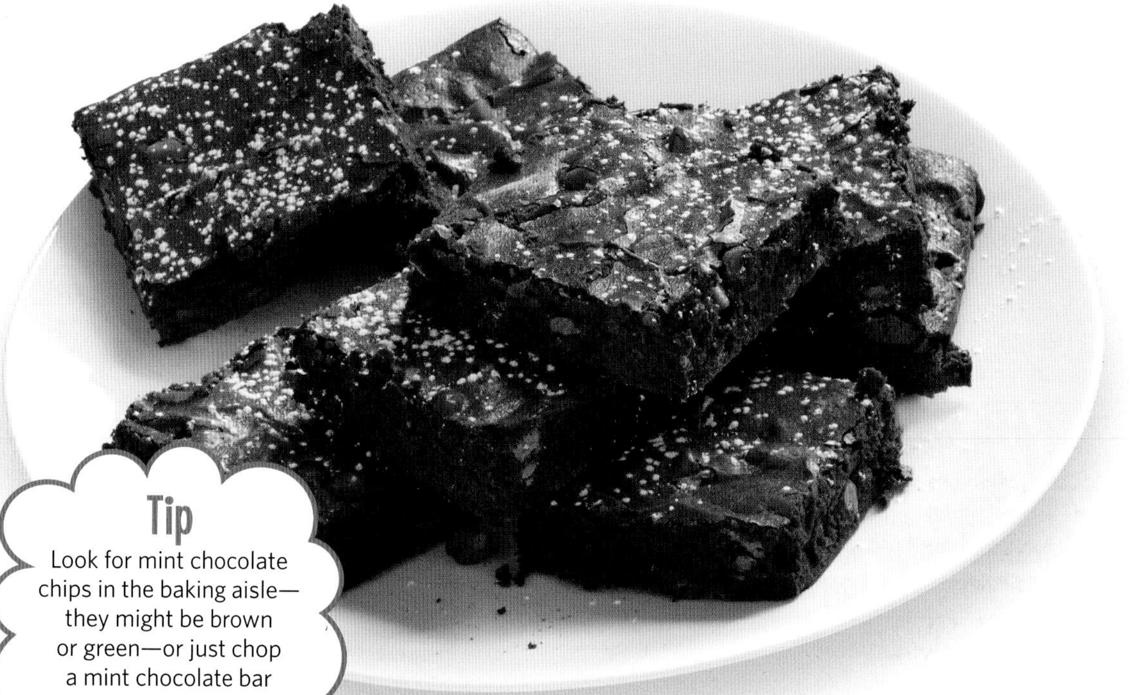

# Mint Brownies

ACTIVE: 25 min TOTAL: 1 hr 10 min (plus cooling) MAKES: 24 to 30

**Cooking spray**
**1½ cups semisweet chocolate chips**
**1 stick unsalted butter**
**¾ cup packed light brown sugar**
**¾ cup granulated sugar**
**4 large eggs**
**1 teaspoon pure vanilla extract**
**1 cup all-purpose flour**
**½ teaspoon salt**
**1 cup mint chocolate chips**
**Confectioners' sugar, for dusting**

1. Preheat the oven to 325°F. Line a 9-by-13-inch baking pan with foil, leaving a 2-inch overhang on two sides. Coat the foil with cooking spray. Melt the chocolate chips and butter in a large saucepan over low heat, stirring with a rubber spatula, until smooth. Remove the pan from the heat.

2. Add the brown sugar and granulated sugar to the chocolate mixture and mix with a whisk, then let cool slightly. Whisk in the eggs, one at a time, then whisk in the vanilla. Mix in the flour and salt. Stir in the mint chips with the rubber spatula.

3. Spread the batter in the pan with the rubber spatula. Bake until a toothpick inserted into the center of the brownies comes out almost clean, about 45 minutes. Remove the pan from the oven with oven mitts, put the pan on a rack and let the brownies cool completely.

4. Lift the brownies out of the pan using the overhanging foil, then peel off the foil. Dust the top of the brownies with confectioners' sugar using a sifter. Cut the brownies into squares.

# Chocolate-Frosted Brownies

ACTIVE: 35 min   TOTAL: 1 hr 5 min (plus cooling)   MAKES: 24 to 30

## FOR THE BROWNIES

Cooking spray

1¾ cups all-purpose flour

3 tablespoons unsweetened cocoa powder

1 teaspoon salt

1 teaspoon baking powder

2 sticks unsalted butter

2½ cups packed light brown sugar

1 cup water

6 ounces unsweetened chocolate, chopped

5 large eggs

2 teaspoons pure vanilla extract

## FOR THE FROSTING

1 stick unsalted butter, at room temperature

1¼ cups confectioners' sugar

3 tablespoons unsweetened cocoa powder

2 tablespoons whole milk, at room temperature

½ teaspoon pure vanilla extract

1. Make the brownies: Preheat the oven to 325°F. Line a 9-by-13-inch baking pan with foil, leaving a 2-inch overhang on two sides. Coat the foil with cooking spray. Mix the flour, cocoa powder, salt and baking powder in a small bowl with a whisk.

2. Combine the butter, brown sugar and water in a large saucepan; bring to a simmer over medium heat, stirring with a whisk. Remove the pan from the heat and whisk in the chopped chocolate until melted. Let cool slightly. Whisk the eggs into the chocolate mixture, one at a time. Stir in the vanilla with a rubber spatula. Stir in the flour mixture until combined.

3. Spread the batter in the pan with the rubber spatula. Bake until a toothpick inserted into the center of the brownies comes out almost clean, 30 to 35 minutes. Remove the pan from the oven with oven mitts, put the pan on a rack and let the brownies cool completely.

4. Meanwhile, make the frosting: Combine the butter, confectioners' sugar, cocoa powder, milk and vanilla in a large bowl. Beat with a mixer on low speed until smooth.

5. Lift the brownies out of the pan using the overhanging foil, then peel off the foil. Spread the frosting on the brownies using an offset spatula or the back of a spoon. Cut the brownies into squares.

# Peanut Butter Cup Brownies

ACTIVE: 25 min    TOTAL: 55 min (plus cooling)    MAKES: 24 to 30

Cooking spray

2  sticks unsalted butter

4  ounces semisweet chocolate, chopped

2  cups sugar

4  large eggs

1½ cups all-purpose flour

⅓  cup unsweetened cocoa powder

½  teaspoon salt

16 peanut butter cups

1 Preheat the oven to 350°F. Line a 9-by-13-inch baking pan with foil, leaving a 2-inch overhang on two sides. Coat the foil with cooking spray. Combine the butter and chocolate in a large saucepan and cook over low heat, stirring occasionally with a rubber spatula, until melted. Remove from the heat and let cool slightly.

2 Add the sugar and eggs to the chocolate mixture and mix with a whisk until smooth. Add the flour, cocoa powder and salt and whisk until combined.

3 Spread the batter in the pan with the rubber spatula. Press the peanut butter cups into the batter with your fingers. Bake until a toothpick inserted into the center of the brownies (but not into a peanut butter cup!) comes out clean, 30 to 35 minutes. Remove the pan from the oven with oven mitts, put the pan on a rack and let the brownies cool completely.

4 Lift the brownies out of the pan using the overhanging foil, then peel off the foil. Cut the brownies into squares.

# Butterscotch Blondies

Cooking spray

2   sticks unsalted butter, melted and cooled

2   cups packed light brown sugar

2   large eggs

1   tablespoon pure vanilla extract

2½ cups all-purpose flour

¼  teaspoon baking soda

¼  teaspoon salt

1½ cups butterscotch chips

1. Preheat the oven to 350°F. Line a 9-by-13-inch baking pan with foil, leaving a 2-inch overhang on two sides. Coat the foil with cooking spray. Combine the melted butter, brown sugar, eggs and vanilla in a large bowl with a whisk. Stir in the flour, baking soda and salt with a wooden spoon. Stir in the butterscotch chips with the spoon.

2. Spread the batter in the pan with a rubber spatula or press in using damp or oiled fingers. Bake until a toothpick inserted into the center of the blondies comes out clean, 30 to 35 minutes. Remove the pan from the oven with oven mitts, put the pan on a rack and let the blondies cool completely.

3. Lift the blondies out of the pan using the overhanging foil, then peel off the foil. Cut the blondies into squares.

## Tip
Blondie batter is pretty thick. If you're having trouble spreading it in the pan, use your fingers: Just dampen them with water or rub them with vegetable oil first.

# Mix Up Your Brownies!

Once you master basic brownies, it's time to start experimenting.

Prepare the batter for Classic Brownies on page 40.
Add one of these mix-ins to the batter and bake.

## Walnuts

Chop 1 cup walnuts and stir into the batter.

## Cookies

Crush enough cookies to equal ½ to 1 cup and stir into the batter.

## Peanut Butter

Swirl ½ cup creamy peanut butter into the batter.

## Pretzels

Line the pan with pretzel sticks before you add the batter.

## Malted Milk Balls

Spread the batter in the pan, then top with chopped malted milk balls before baking.

## Coconut

Spread 1 cup sweetened shredded coconut on a baking sheet. Bake at 325°F until golden, 8 to 10 minutes, stirring once. Let cool, then add to the batter.

## Butterscotch Chips

Add ¾ cup to the batter.

## Cherries

Add ½ cup chopped maraschino cherries to the batter.

## Jam

Swirl ½ cup jam (any flavor) into the batter.

## M&M's

Add ½ to 1 cup to the batter.

## Chocolate Chips

Add ¾ cup to the batter.

## Toffee Bits

Add ½ cup to the batter.

## Chile Powder

Add ½ teaspoon ancho chile powder to the batter.

## Sesame Seeds

Add 1 tablespoon toasted sesame seeds to the batter.

## Marshmallows

Top the brownies with mini marshmallows during the last 10 minutes of baking.

# Snickerdoodle Bars

ACTIVE: 25 min    TOTAL: 50 min (plus cooling)    MAKES: 24 to 30

Cooking spray

2    sticks unsalted butter, melted and cooled slightly

1¾  cups sugar

3    large eggs

1    tablespoon pure vanilla extract

2    cups all-purpose flour

1½  teaspoons cream of tartar

¼    teaspoon salt

1    tablespoon ground cinnamon

1 Preheat the oven to 350°F. Line a 9-by-13-inch baking pan with foil, leaving a 2-inch overhang on two sides. Coat the foil with cooking spray. Combine the melted butter, 1½ cups sugar, the eggs and vanilla in a large bowl with a whisk. Stir in the flour, cream of tartar and salt with a wooden spoon until combined.

2 Spread the dough in the pan with a rubber spatula or press in using damp or oiled fingers. Mix the remaining ¼ cup sugar with the cinnamon in a small bowl, then sprinkle the cinnamon sugar on top of the dough. Bake until the edges of the bars are set but the center is soft, about 25 minutes. Remove the pan from the oven with oven mitts, put the pan on a rack and let the bars cool completely.

3 Lift the bars out of the pan using the overhanging foil, then peel off the foil. Cut into squares.

## Tip
When you're making these, mix some extra cinnamon sugar to sprinkle on buttered toast: ¼ cup sugar and 1 tablespoon ground cinnamon is a good ratio.

# Trail Mix Bars

ACTIVE: 25 min    TOTAL: 45 min (plus cooling)    MAKES: 24 to 30

Cooking spray

**3**   **cups rolled oats**

**½**   **cup salted peanuts**

**½**   **cup salted sunflower seeds**

**6**   **tablespoons unsalted butter**

**⅔**   **cup packed light brown sugar**

**½**   **cup honey**

**2**   **teaspoons pure vanilla extract**

**1**   **teaspoon salt**

**½**   **cup raisins**

**½**   **cup mini M&M's**

1. Preheat the oven to 350°F. Line a 9-by-13-inch baking pan with foil, leaving a 2-inch overhang on two sides. Coat the foil with cooking spray. Spread the oats, peanuts and sunflower seeds on a rimmed baking sheet. Bake until toasted, about 10 minutes. Remove from the oven with oven mitts and set aside.

2. Meanwhile, combine the butter, brown sugar, honey, vanilla and salt in a small saucepan. Cook over medium heat, stirring with a wooden spoon, until the butter is melted and the sugar is dissolved. Remove from the heat and stir in the oat mixture. Let cool slightly, then stir in the raisins and M&M's.

3. Spread the mixture in the pan with a rubber spatula or press in using damp or oiled fingers. Bake until lightly browned, about 20 minutes. Remove the pan from the oven with oven mitts, then put the pan on a rack and let the bars cool completely.

4. Lift the bars out of the pan using the overhanging foil, then peel off the foil. Cut into squares.

## Did You Know?

Many people call trail mix gorp, but no one can agree on what it means. Some say it stands for Good Old Raisins and Peanuts; others claim it means Granola, Oats, Raisins and Peanuts.

# Triple-Decker Bars

ACTIVE: 40 min    TOTAL: 1½ hr (plus cooling)    MAKES: 24 to 30

## FOR THE BROWNIES

Cooking spray

| | |
|---|---|
| 2 | sticks unsalted butter |
| 4 | ounces chopped semisweet chocolate |
| 2 | cups sugar |
| 4 | large eggs |
| 1½ | cups all-purpose flour |
| ⅓ | cup unsweetened cocoa powder |
| ½ | teaspoon salt |

## FOR THE BLONDIES

| | |
|---|---|
| 2 | sticks unsalted butter, melted and cooled |
| 2 | cups packed light brown sugar |
| 2 | large eggs |
| 1 | tablespoon pure vanilla extract |
| 2½ | cups all-purpose flour |
| ¼ | teaspoon baking soda |
| ¼ | teaspoon salt |
| 1½ | cups butterscotch chips |
| 30 to 35 | chocolate sandwich cookies |

1. Preheat the oven to 350°F. Line a 9-by-13-inch baking pan with foil, leaving a 2-inch overhang on two sides. Coat the foil with cooking spray.

2. Make the brownie batter: Combine the butter and chocolate in a large saucepan and cook over low heat, stirring occasionally with a rubber spatula, until melted. Remove from the heat and let cool slightly. Add the sugar and eggs to the chocolate mixture and stir with a whisk. Add the flour, cocoa powder and salt and whisk until combined.

3. Make the blondie batter: Combine the melted butter, brown sugar, eggs and vanilla in a large bowl with a whisk. Add the flour, baking soda and salt and stir with a wooden spoon. Stir in the butterscotch chips with the spoon.

4. Spread the brownie batter in the pan with the rubber spatula. Press a single layer of chocolate sandwich cookies into the top. Carefully spread the blondie batter over the cookies.

5. Bake until a toothpick inserted into the center of the bars comes out clean, 50 to 55 minutes. Remove the pan from the oven with oven mitts, put the pan on a rack and let the bars cool completely.

6. Lift the bars out of the pan using the overhanging foil, then peel off the foil. Cut into squares.

**Did You Know?**

Some say that the first pretzels were called pretiola in Latin, which means "little rewards." The name is fitting, don't you think?

# Butterscotch Pretzel Bars

ACTIVE: 30 min    TOTAL: 1 hr (plus cooling)    MAKES: 24 to 30

Cooking spray

2   sticks unsalted butter, melted and cooled

2   cups packed light brown sugar

2   large eggs

1   tablespoon pure vanilla extract

2½ cups all-purpose flour

¼   teaspoon baking soda

¼   teaspoon salt

1½ cups butterscotch chips

½   cup butterscotch sauce

1   cup broken pretzel sticks

1   Preheat the oven to 350°F. Line a 9-by-13-inch baking pan with foil, leaving a 2-inch overhang on two sides. Coat the foil with cooking spray. Combine the melted butter, brown sugar, eggs and vanilla in a large bowl with a whisk. Add the flour, baking soda and salt and stir with a wooden spoon. Stir in the butterscotch chips with the spoon.

2   Spread the batter in the pan using a rubber spatula or press in using damp or oiled fingers. Drizzle with the butterscotch sauce and swirl it in with a butter knife. Top evenly with the pretzel sticks.

3   Bake until a toothpick inserted into the center of the bars comes out clean, 30 to 35 minutes. Remove the pan from the oven with oven mitts, put the pan on a rack and let the bars cool completely.

4   Lift the bars out of the pan using the overhanging foil, then peel off the foil. Cut into squares.

# Chocolate-Pecan Bars

ACTIVE: 30 min    TOTAL: 55 min (plus cooling)    MAKES: about 24

## FOR THE CRUST

Cooking spray

⅓   cup pecans

2   cups all-purpose flour

½   cup granulated sugar

½   teaspoon salt

1½  sticks (12 tablespoons) cold unsalted butter, cut into cubes

## FOR THE TOPPING

¾   cup dark corn syrup

½   cup granulated sugar

½   cup packed light brown sugar

4   large eggs

4   tablespoons unsalted butter, melted

2   teaspoons pure vanilla extract

Pinch of salt

1½  cups pecans, roughly chopped

3   ounces bittersweet chocolate, roughly chopped

1. Make the crust: Preheat the oven to 350°F. Line a 9-by-13-inch baking pan with foil, leaving a 2-inch overhang on two sides. Coat the foil with cooking spray. Pulse the pecans in a food processor until finely ground. Add the flour, granulated sugar and salt and pulse to combine. Add the cold butter and pulse until the dough starts clumping together (it will still be crumbly).

2. Dump the dough into the pan and press into an even layer with your fingers. Bake until golden brown and set, 25 to 30 minutes. Remove the pan from the oven with oven mitts.

3. Meanwhile, make the topping: Whisk the corn syrup, granulated sugar, brown sugar, eggs, melted butter, vanilla and salt in a large bowl until smooth. Stir in the pecans.

4. Spread the topping over the warm crust and sprinkle evenly with the chocolate. Return to the oven and bake until the top is set and no longer jiggly, 25 to 30 minutes. Remove the pan from the oven with oven mitts, then put the pan on a rack and let the bars cool completely.

5. Lift the bars out of the pan using the overhanging foil, then peel off the foil. Cut into diamonds or squares.

**Did You Know?**
Albany, GA, calls itself the pecan capital of America—it's home to more than 600,000 pecan trees!

# Birthday Cake Bars

ACTIVE: 25 min    TOTAL: 50 min (plus cooling)    MAKES: 24 to 30

Cooking spray

2 sticks unsalted butter, melted and cooled slightly

1½ cups sugar

3 large eggs

1 tablespoon pure vanilla extract

2 cups all-purpose flour

¼ teaspoon salt

½ cup rainbow sprinkles, plus more for topping

Vanilla frosting, for topping

1 Preheat the oven to 350°F. Line a 9-by-13-inch baking pan with foil, leaving a 2-inch overhang on two sides. Coat the foil with cooking spray. Combine the melted butter, sugar, eggs and vanilla in a large bowl with a whisk. Stir in the flour and salt with a wooden spoon until combined. Stir in the sprinkles with the spoon.

2 Spread the batter in the pan with a rubber spatula or press in using damp or oiled fingers. Bake until the edges of the bars are set but the center is soft, about 25 minutes. Remove the pan from the oven with oven mitts, then put the pan on a rack and let the bars cool completely.

3 Lift the bars out of the pan using the overhanging foil, then peel off the foil. Spread frosting on top with an offset spatula or the back of a spoon. Top with more sprinkles. Cut into squares.

## Tip

You can use store-bought frosting for these bars, or try our frosting recipe on page 100. You can skip the frosting, too. The bars will still taste great!

# Chocolate Chip Cookie Bars

ACTIVE: 20 min    TOTAL: 55 min (plus cooling)    MAKES: 24 to 30

Cooking spray

2   sticks unsalted butter, at room temperature

1   cup granulated sugar

1   cup packed light brown sugar

3   large eggs

1½  teaspoons pure vanilla extract

3   cups all-purpose flour

¾   teaspoon baking soda

¾   teaspoon salt

1   12-ounce bag semisweet chocolate chips

1. Preheat the oven to 350°F. Line a 9-by-13-inch baking pan with foil, leaving a 2-inch overhang on two sides. Coat the foil with cooking spray. Combine the butter, granulated sugar and brown sugar in a large bowl. Beat with a mixer on medium-high speed until fluffy, about 2 minutes. Beat in the eggs and vanilla. Reduce the mixer speed to low and add the flour, baking soda and salt; beat until combined. Stir in the chocolate chips with a wooden spoon.

2. Spread the dough in the pan with a rubber spatula or press in using damp or oiled fingers. Bake until a toothpick inserted into the center of the bars comes out clean, 35 to 40 minutes. Remove the pan from the oven with oven mitts, then put the pan on a rack and let the bars cool completely.

3. Lift the bars out of the pan using the overhanging foil, then peel off the foil. Cut into squares.

# Sweet-and-Salty Snack Bars

ACTIVE: 15 min    TOTAL: 45 min (plus cooling)    MAKES: 24 to 30

**Cooking spray**

2  cups crushed potato chips

2  cups salted peanuts

1  cup shredded sweetened coconut

1  cup semisweet chocolate chips

1  cup raisins

1  cup toffee bits

1  14-ounce can sweetened condensed milk

1   Preheat the oven to 350°F. Line a 9-by-13-inch baking pan with foil, leaving a 2-inch overhang on two sides. Coat the foil with cooking spray. Toss together the potato chips, peanuts, coconut, chocolate chips, raisins and toffee bits in a large bowl with a wooden spoon.

2   Gently press the mixture into the pan with your fingers. Pour the condensed milk all over the top. Bake until bubbling around the edges, about 30 minutes. Remove the pan from the oven with oven mitts, then put the pan on a rack and let the bars cool completely.

3   Lift the bars out of the pan using the overhanging foil, then peel off the foil. Cut into squares.

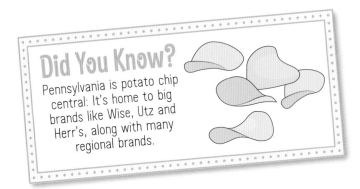

## Did You Know?

Pennsylvania is potato chip central: It's home to big brands like Wise, Utz and Herr's, along with many regional brands.

# Gluten-Free Peanut Butter-Chocolate Bars

ACTIVE: 30 min    TOTAL: 1 hr (plus cooling)    MAKES: 24 to 30

## FOR THE BARS

Cooking spray

3  cups creamy peanut butter

2  cups sugar

3  large eggs

2  teaspoons pure
   vanilla extract

1  teaspoon salt

## FOR THE FROSTING

½  cup heavy cream

6  ounces semisweet
   chocolate, chopped

1  tablespoon unsalted butter

Pinch of salt

1  Make the bars: Preheat the oven to 350°F. Line a 9-by-13-inch baking pan with foil, leaving a 2-inch overhang on two sides. Coat the foil with cooking spray. Combine the peanut butter, sugar, eggs, vanilla and salt in a large bowl. Beat with a mixer on medium speed until smooth.

2  Spread the batter in the pan with a rubber spatula or press in using damp or oiled fingers. Bake until a toothpick inserted into the center comes out clean, 30 to 35 minutes. Remove the pan from the oven with oven mitts, then put the pan on a rack and let the bars cool completely.

3  Meanwhile, make the frosting: Heat the heavy cream in a small saucepan over medium-high heat until just simmering. Combine the chocolate, butter and salt in a large bowl. Pour the warm heavy cream over the chocolate mixture and stir with a whisk until smooth.

4  Lift the bars out of the pan using the overhanging foil, then peel off the foil. Spread the frosting on top of the bars with an offset spatula and refrigerate until set. Cut into squares.

## Did You Know?

Peanut butter is naturally gluten-free, but you should check the label. Some brands contain traces of gluten.

**Tip**

This recipe is a great way to use up an overripe banana. Brown spots on the peel are a good thing: They mean the banana is extra soft and sweet!

# Chunky Monkey Bars

ACTIVE: 25 min    TOTAL: 1 hr (plus cooling)    MAKES: 24 to 30

Cooking spray

3   cups all-purpose flour

¾   teaspoon salt

2   sticks unsalted butter,
    at room temperature

1   cup granulated sugar

1   cup packed
    dark brown sugar

3   large eggs

1   overripe banana,
    mashed with a fork

2   teaspoons pure
    vanilla extract

1   cup semisweet
    chocolate chips

1   cup chopped walnuts

1. Preheat the oven to 350°F. Line a 9-by-13-inch baking pan with foil, leaving a 2-inch overhang on two sides. Coat the foil with cooking spray. Mix the flour and salt in a medium bowl with a whisk.

2. Combine the butter, granulated sugar and brown sugar in a large bowl. Beat with a mixer on medium-high speed until creamy, about 2 minutes. Add the eggs, mashed banana and vanilla and beat until combined. Beat in the flour mixture until just combined, then stir in the chocolate chips and walnuts with a wooden spoon.

3. Spread the batter in the pan with a rubber spatula. Bake until a toothpick inserted into the center of the bars comes out clean, 35 to 40 minutes. Remove the pan from the oven with oven mitts, then put the pan on a rack and let the bars cool completely.

4. Lift the bars out of the pan using the overhanging foil, then peel off the foil. Cut into squares.

## Did You Know?

Banana pairs well with chocolate and walnuts: It's the flavor combination in one of Ben & Jerry's best-selling flavors, Chunky Monkey!

# Sugar Cookie Bars

ACTIVE: 25 min    TOTAL: 50 min (plus cooling)    MAKES: 24 to 30

Cooking spray

2   **sticks unsalted butter, melted and cooled slightly**

1½   **cups sugar**

3   **large eggs**

1   **tablespoon pure vanilla extract**

2   **cups all-purpose flour**

¼   **teaspoon salt**

1   Preheat the oven to 350°F. Line a 9-by-13-inch baking pan with foil, leaving a 2-inch overhang on two sides. Coat the foil with cooking spray. Combine the melted butter, sugar, eggs and vanilla in a large bowl with a whisk. Stir in the flour and salt with a wooden spoon until combined.

2   Spread the batter in the pan with a rubber spatula or press in using damp or oiled fingers. Bake until the edges of the bars are set but the center is soft, about 25 minutes. Remove the pan from the oven with oven mitts, then put the pan on a rack and let the bars cool completely.

3   Lift the bars out of the pan using the overhanging foil, then peel off the foil. Cut into squares.

## Did You Know?

Sugar cookies have a pretty straightforward name, but early versions of the cookie were called crybabies, gemmels, jumbles and plunkets!

# Confetti Magic Bars

ACTIVE: 20 min    TOTAL: 55 min (plus cooling)    MAKES: 24 to 30

**Vegetable oil, for the pan**

**1**  stick unsalted butter, melted

**2**  cups graham cracker crumbs

**1**  14-ounce can sweetened condensed milk

**1**  cup chopped pecans

**1**  cup sweetened shredded coconut

**1**  cup butterscotch chips

**1**  cup dark chocolate chips

**¼**  cup rainbow sprinkles

1  Preheat the oven to 350°F. Coat a 9-by-13-inch baking pan with vegetable oil. Mix the melted butter and graham cracker crumbs in a medium bowl with a wooden spoon. Press the mixture into the pan with your fingers.

2  Pour the condensed milk over the crumb mixture. Top with the pecans, coconut, butterscotch chips and chocolate chips. Scatter the sprinkles on top.

3  Bake until the bars are golden around the edges, 35 to 40 minutes. Remove the pan from the oven with oven mitts, then put the pan on a rack and let the bars cool completely. Cut into squares.

# Oatmeal-Raisin Cookie Bars

ACTIVE: 20 min    TOTAL: 55 min (plus cooling)    MAKES: 24 to 30

Cooking spray

2   sticks unsalted butter,
    at room temperature
¾   cup granulated sugar
¾   cup packed light
    brown sugar
2½  cups rolled oats
1½  cups all-purpose flour
1   teaspoon baking powder
1   teaspoon salt
2   cups raisins
2   large eggs
2   teaspoons pure
    vanilla extract

1  Preheat the oven to 350°F. Line a 9-by-13-inch baking pan with foil, leaving a 2-inch overhang on two sides. Coat the foil with cooking spray. Combine the butter, granulated sugar and brown sugar in a food processor. Pulse until well mixed. Add the oats, flour, baking powder and salt and pulse to combine. Add the raisins, eggs and vanilla and pulse until large clumps form.

2  Spread the dough in the pan with a rubber spatula or press in using damp or oiled fingers. Bake until the edges are set but the center is soft, about 35 minutes. Remove the pan from the oven with oven mitts, then put the pan on a rack and let the bars cool completely.

3  Lift the bars out of the pan using the overhanging foil, then peel off the foil. Cut into squares.

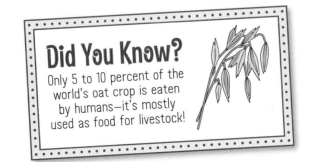

### Did You Know?
Only 5 to 10 percent of the world's oat crop is eaten by humans—it's mostly used as food for livestock!

# Lemon Bars

ACTIVE: 25 min    TOTAL: 1 hr 5 min (plus cooling)    MAKES: 24 to 30

**Cooking spray**

**2⅓ cups all-purpose flour**

**¾ cup confectioners' sugar, plus more for dusting**

**Pinch of salt**

**2 sticks unsalted butter, at room temperature**

**5 large eggs**

**1½ cups granulated sugar**

**1 cup fresh lemon juice**

1. Preheat the oven to 350°F. Line a 9-by-13-inch baking pan with foil, leaving a 2-inch overhang on two sides. Coat the foil with cooking spray. Mix 2 cups flour, the confectioners' sugar and salt in a large bowl with a whisk. Work in the butter with your fingers until large clumps form.

2. Press the crust mixture into the pan in an even layer. Bake until lightly browned, 20 to 25 minutes. Remove the pan from the oven with mitts, then put the pan on a rack and let cool 5 minutes.

3. Meanwhile, combine the eggs, granulated sugar, lemon juice and remaining ⅓ cup flour in a large bowl and mix with a whisk until smooth. Pour the lemon mixture over the warm crust.

4. Bake until the lemon bars are set, 20 to 25 minutes. Remove the pan from the oven with oven mitts, then put the pan on the rack and let the bars cool completely.

5. Lift the bars out of the pan using the overhanging foil, then peel off the foil. Dust the tops of the bars with confectioners' sugar using a sifter. Cut into squares.

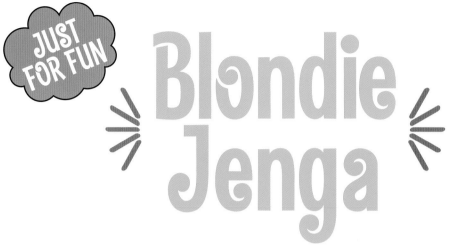

# Blondie Jenga

Turn your favorite treats into a game!

## How to Make a Cookie Tower

**1** Choose a firm, stable cookie, like the Chocolate Chip Cookie Bars on page 57 or the Butterscotch Blondies on page 47. Cut into rectangles.

**2** Stack the bars like a game of Jenga—lay 3 bars next to each other, then top with 3 more bars in the opposite direction. Repeat to make a tower.

**3** Try to remove the bars without knocking down the tower. Or just grab a bar and eat it!

cookies

## Did You Know?

White chocolate isn't really chocolate! It doesn't contain any chocolate solids—just milk products, sugar, cocoa butter, vanilla and additives. But we love it all the same!

# Red Velvet– White Chocolate Chip Cookies

ACTIVE: **25 min**   TOTAL: **1 hr 10 min (plus cooling)**   MAKES: **about 36**

- **2** cups all-purpose flour
- **2** tablespoons unsweetened cocoa powder
- **½** teaspoon baking soda
- **½** teaspoon baking powder
- **½** teaspoon salt
- **1** stick unsalted butter, at room temperature
- **½** cup granulated sugar
- **½** cup packed light brown sugar
- **2** large eggs, at room temperature
- **1** teaspoon pure vanilla extract
- **¼** cup sour cream
- **2** teaspoons red gel food coloring
- **1½** cups white chocolate chips

**1** Preheat the oven to 375°F. Line 2 baking sheets with parchment paper. Mix the flour, cocoa powder, baking soda, baking powder and salt in a medium bowl with a whisk.

**2** Beat the butter, granulated sugar and brown sugar in a large bowl with a mixer on medium-high speed until pale and fluffy, about 3 minutes. Beat in the eggs, one at a time, then beat in the vanilla. Reduce the mixer speed to low; beat in half of the flour mixture until just combined. Beat in the sour cream and food coloring, then beat in the remaining flour mixture. Stir in the chocolate chips with a wooden spoon. Refrigerate the dough until firm, 30 minutes to 1 hour.

**3** Scoop heaping tablespoonfuls of dough 2 inches apart onto the baking sheets. Bake until the cookies are puffed in the middle and set around the edges, 8 to 12 minutes. Remove the pans from the oven with oven mitts. Let the cookies cool 5 minutes on the pans, then use a spatula to move the cookies to racks to cool completely.

# Snack Attack Cookies with Bacon

ACTIVE: **45 min**    TOTAL: **1 hr (plus cooling)**    MAKES: **about 24**

- 5 slices bacon, chopped
- ½ cup plus 2 teaspoons packed dark brown sugar
- 1 teaspoon water
- 1½ cups all-purpose flour
- ½ teaspoon baking powder
- ½ teaspoon baking soda
- ¼ teaspoon salt
- 1¼ sticks (10 tablespoons) unsalted butter, at room temperature
- ½ cup granulated sugar
- 1 large egg plus 1 egg yolk, at room temperature
- 2 teaspoons pure vanilla extract
- 1 cup broken mini pretzels
- ½ cup semisweet chocolate chips
- ½ cup mini M&M's
- 2 cups potato chips, broken

**1** Preheat the oven to 350˚F. Line 2 baking sheets with parchment paper. Cook the bacon in a medium skillet over medium heat, stirring occasionally, until crisp, about 10 minutes. Carefully pour the drippings into a small bowl, keeping the bacon in the skillet; let the drippings cool.

**2** Add 2 teaspoons brown sugar and the water to the skillet with the bacon and cook, stirring, until the sugar dissolves and the bacon is crisp, about 1 minute. Remove the bacon and put on a plate to cool.

**3** Mix the flour, baking powder, baking soda and salt in a medium bowl with a whisk. In a large bowl, beat the butter, 2 tablespoons of the reserved bacon drippings, the remaining ½ cup brown sugar and the granulated sugar with a mixer on medium-high speed until light and fluffy, 2 to 3 minutes. Beat in the whole egg, egg yolk and vanilla until well combined. Reduce the mixer speed to low and beat in the flour mixture until just combined. Add the pretzels, chocolate chips, M&M's and bacon and beat until just combined. Stir in the potato chips with a rubber spatula.

**4** Roll the dough into large balls (about 3 tablespoons each). Place 2 inches apart on the baking sheets. Bake until the cookies are set around the edges but soft in the middle, 13 to 15 minutes. Remove the pans from the oven with oven mitts. Let the cookies cool 5 minutes on the pans, then use a spatula to move the cookies to racks to cool completely.

## Tip
To make the bacon easier to chop, pop it in the freezer for 10 to 15 minutes first.

# Pumpkin Spice Chocolate Chip Cookies

ACTIVE: **30 min**   TOTAL: **50 min (plus cooling)**   MAKES: **about 24**

- 2½ cups all-purpose flour
- 1½ teaspoons pumpkin pie spice
- ½ teaspoon baking soda
- ½ teaspoon baking powder
- ½ teaspoon salt
- 2 sticks unsalted butter, melted and cooled
- 2 large eggs
- ¾ cup granulated sugar
- ¾ cup packed light brown sugar
- 1 teaspoon pure vanilla extract
- 1½ cups semisweet chocolate chips

**1** Preheat the oven to 350°F. Line 2 baking sheets with parchment paper. Mix the flour, pumpkin pie spice, baking soda, baking powder and salt in a large bowl with a whisk.

**2** Whisk the melted butter, eggs, granulated sugar, brown sugar and vanilla in a medium bowl. Stir the butter mixture into the flour mixture with a wooden spoon. Stir in the chocolate chips.

**3** Scoop heaping tablespoonfuls of dough about 2 inches apart onto the baking sheets. Bake until the cookies are golden, 16 to 18 minutes. Remove the pans from the oven with oven mitts. Let the cookies cool 5 minutes on the pans, then use a spatula to move the cookies to racks to cool completely.

## Did You Know?

Starbucks introduced the pumpkin spice latte in 2003 and started an obsession: The chain has since sold more than 420 million PSLs!

# Loaded Chocolate Cookies

ACTIVE: **30 min**     TOTAL: **45 min (plus cooling)**     MAKES: **about 18**

**2½ cups all-purpose flour**

**1    teaspoon baking soda**

**¾   teaspoon salt**

**2    sticks unsalted butter, melted and cooled slightly**

**1½ cups packed light brown sugar**

**½   cup unsweetened cocoa powder**

**2    large eggs, lightly beaten**

**1½ teaspoons pure vanilla extract**

**½   cup bittersweet chocolate chips**

**2    cups mix-ins (such as M&M's, toffee bits, shredded coconut, peanut butter chips and/or white chocolate chunks)**

**1** Preheat the oven to 375˚F. Line 2 baking sheets with parchment paper. Mix the flour, baking soda and salt in a large bowl with a whisk.

**2** In a separate large bowl, combine the melted butter, brown sugar, cocoa powder, eggs and vanilla with the whisk. Stir the flour mixture into the butter mixture with a wooden spoon, then stir in the bittersweet chocolate chips and other mix-ins.

**3** Scoop tablespoonfuls of dough about 3 inches apart onto the baking sheets; smooth the tops with damp fingers. Bake until the cookies are puffed and set, about 12 minutes. Remove the pans from the oven with oven mitts. Let the cookies cool 5 minutes on the pans, then use a spatula to move the cookies to racks to cool completely.

# Triple Chocolate-Hazelnut Cookies

ACTIVE: **30 min**    TOTAL: **45 min (plus cooling)**    MAKES: **about 24**

1    **cup blanched hazelnuts, chopped**

⅓    **cup all-purpose flour**

½    **teaspoon baking powder**

¼    **teaspoon salt**

8    **ounces bittersweet chocolate, chopped**

6    **tablespoons unsalted butter**

1    **teaspoon pure vanilla extract**

2    **large eggs**

¾    **cup sugar**

1    **cup milk chocolate chips**

1    **cup white chocolate chips**

**1** Preheat the oven to 350°F. Spread the nuts on a baking sheet and bake until golden, about 7 minutes. Remove the pan from the oven with oven mitts. Line 2 other baking sheets with parchment paper.

**2** Mix the flour, baking powder and salt in a medium bowl with a whisk. Combine the chopped chocolate and butter in a microwave-safe bowl and microwave 30 seconds at a time, stirring, until melted. Add the vanilla and whisk until smooth.

**3** Beat the eggs in a large bowl with a mixer on medium speed until foamy, about 1 minute. Gradually add the sugar and beat until thick and pale yellow, about 6 minutes. Gradually add the melted chocolate mixture and beat until combined. Reduce the mixer speed to low; add the flour mixture and beat until just combined, about 1 minute. Stir in the hazelnuts and chocolate chips with a wooden spoon.

**4** Scoop heaping tablespoonfuls of dough about 2 inches apart onto the baking sheets. Bake until the cookies are slightly puffed and crackly, 12 to 15 minutes. Remove the pans from the oven with oven mitts. Let the cookies cool 5 minutes on the pans, then use a spatula to move the cookies to racks to cool completely.

## Did You Know?
Oregon is one of the few states with an official state nut: the hazelnut. The state produces 99 percent of America's hazelnuts!

# Confetti Biscotti

ACTIVE: **30 min**     TOTAL: **1 hr 15 min (plus cooling)**     MAKES: **about 24**

2½ cups all-purpose flour

2 teaspoons baking powder

¼ teaspoon salt

1 stick unsalted butter, at room temperature

1 cup sugar

2 large eggs

2 teaspoons pure vanilla extract

½ cup sprinkles, plus more for topping

4 ounces white chocolate, chopped

**1** Line a baking sheet with parchment paper. Mix the flour, baking powder and salt in a medium bowl with a whisk.

**2** Beat the butter and sugar in a large bowl with a mixer on medium speed until fluffy, about 3 minutes. Beat in the eggs, one at a time, then the vanilla. With the mixer on low speed, beat in the flour mixture until just combined. Stir in the sprinkles with a wooden spoon.

**3** Form the dough with your hands into two 8-inch logs (2½ inches wide). Place on the baking sheet, leaving space between them. Refrigerate 30 minutes.

**4** Preheat the oven to 350°F. Bake until the logs are cooked through, 25 to 30 minutes. Remove the pan from the oven with oven mitts; let cool slightly.

**5** Reduce the oven temperature to 300°F. Slide the dough logs onto a cutting board and slice crosswise ½ inch thick with a sharp knife. Place the pieces cut-side down on the baking sheet and return to the oven. Bake until crisp, about 20 minutes. Remove the pan from the oven with oven mitts. Let the biscotti cool completely on the pan.

**6** Meanwhile, put the white chocolate in a medium microwave-safe bowl and microwave 30 seconds at a time, stirring, until melted. Scrape into a resealable plastic bag and snip a corner. Drizzle the white chocolate on the biscotti. Top with more sprinkles.

## Did You Know?

Biscotti are super-crunchy cookies— they're baked two times! The word biscotti means "twice baked" in Italian.

## Tip

You can buy a box of graham cracker crumbs or just crush them yourself: Put 4 graham cracker sheets in a resealable plastic bag and smash them with a rolling pin.

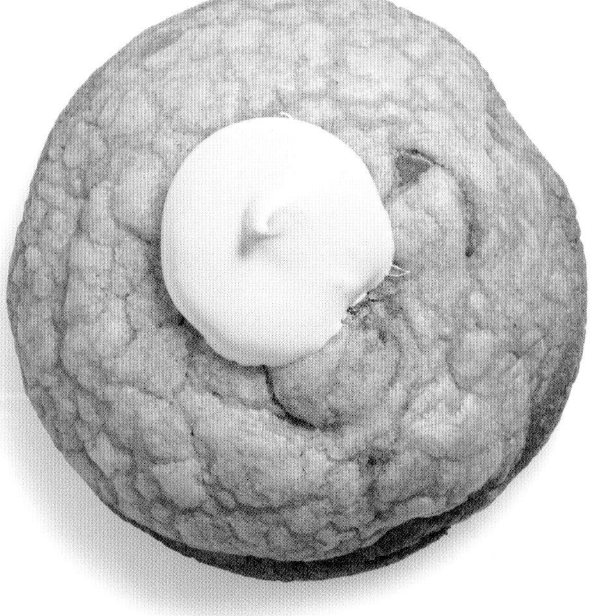

# S'mores Chocolate Chip Cookies

ACTIVE: **30 min** TOTAL: **45 min (plus cooling)** MAKES: **about 24**

- **1¼ cups all-purpose flour**
- **½ cup fine graham cracker crumbs**
- **¾ teaspoon baking soda**
- **½ teaspoon salt**
- **1¼ sticks (10 tablespoons) unsalted butter, at room temperature**
- **1 cup packed light brown sugar**
- **1 large egg, at room temperature**
- **1 teaspoon pure vanilla extract**
- **1 cup milk chocolate chips**
- **Marshmallow cream, for topping**

**1** Preheat the oven to 375°F. Line 2 baking sheets with parchment paper. Mix the flour, graham cracker crumbs, baking soda and salt in a medium bowl with a whisk.

**2** In a large bowl, beat the butter and brown sugar with a mixer on medium-high speed until pale and fluffy, about 4 minutes. Beat in the egg and vanilla. Reduce the mixer speed to low and beat in the flour mixture until just combined. Stir in the chocolate chips with a wooden spoon.

**3** Roll the dough into 1½-inch balls and place 2 inches apart on the baking sheets. Bake until the cookies are set around the edges, 12 to 15 minutes. Remove the pans from the oven with oven mitts. Let the cookies cool 10 minutes on the pans.

**4** Fill a plastic bag with marshmallow cream and snip a corner. Pipe the marshmallow cream on the warm cookies. Use a spatula to move the cookies to racks to set and cool completely.

# Chocolate-Raspberry Cookies

ACTIVE: **30 min**    TOTAL: **45 min (plus cooling)**    MAKES: **about 36**

- 1½ **cups all-purpose flour**
- ¼ **cup unsweetened dark cocoa powder**
- ¾ **teaspoon baking soda**
- ½ **teaspoon salt**
- 1¼ **sticks (10 tablespoons) unsalted butter, at room temperature**
- 1 **cup packed light brown sugar**
- 1 **large egg, at room temperature**
- 1 **teaspoon pure vanilla extract**
- ¾ **cup semisweet chocolate chips**
- ½ **cup white chocolate chips**
- ½ **cup crushed freeze-dried raspberries**

**1** Preheat the oven to 375°F. Line 2 baking sheets with parchment paper. Mix the flour, cocoa powder, baking soda and salt in a medium bowl with a whisk.

**2** In a large bowl, beat the butter and brown sugar with a mixer on medium-high speed until well combined, about 4 minutes. Beat in the egg and vanilla. Beat in the flour mixture on low speed. Stir in the semisweet and white chocolate chips and the freeze-dried raspberries with a wooden spoon.

**3** Roll the dough into 1½-inch balls and place 2 inches apart on the baking sheets. Bake until the cookies are just set, 12 to 15 minutes. Remove the pans from the oven with oven mitts. Let the cookies cool 5 minutes on the pans, then use a spatula to move the cookies to racks to cool completely.

## Did You Know?

The average person in the United States eats about 35,000 cookies in a lifetime. How many do you think you've had so far?

# Chocolate-Mint Chip Cookies

ACTIVE: **30 min**　TOTAL: **45 min (plus cooling)**　MAKES: **about 36**

- 1½ **cups all-purpose flour**
- ¼ **cup unsweetened dark cocoa powder**
- 1 **teaspoon baking soda**
- ¾ **teaspoon salt**
- 1 **stick unsalted butter, at room temperature**
- 1 **cup superfine sugar**
- ¼ **cup packed dark brown sugar**
- ¼ **cup vegetable oil**
- 1 **teaspoon water**
- ½ **teaspoon peppermint extract**
- 2 **large eggs, at room temperature**
- 1½ **cups chopped mint chocolate**
- 4 **ounces white chocolate, chopped**
- 2 **teaspoons coconut oil**
- 1 to 2 **drops green liquid food coloring**

**1** Preheat the oven to 350°F. Line 2 baking sheets with parchment paper. Mix the flour, cocoa powder, baking soda and salt in a medium bowl with a whisk.

**2** In a large bowl, beat the butter, superfine sugar, brown sugar and vegetable oil with a mixer on medium speed until creamy, 2 to 4 minutes. Beat in the water and peppermint extract until smooth. Beat in the eggs, one at a time. Reduce the mixer speed to low and beat in the flour mixture until just combined. Stir in the chopped mint chocolate with a wooden spoon.

**3** Scoop heaping tablespoonfuls of dough about 3 inches apart on the baking sheets. Bake until the cookies are mostly set, 15 to 20 minutes. Remove the pans from the oven with oven mitts. Let the cookies cool completely on the pans.

**4** Make the glaze: Put the white chocolate and coconut oil in a microwave-safe bowl and microwave 30 seconds at a time, stirring, until melted. Stir in the green food coloring. Drizzle the glaze over the cooled cookies using a fork.

# Chewy Ginger Cookies

ACTIVE: **30 min**   TOTAL: **45 min (plus cooling)**   MAKES: **about 30**

1   **stick unsalted butter, at room temperature, plus more for the pans**

2½ **cups all-purpose flour**

1   **teaspoon baking soda**

1   **teaspoon ground ginger**

¼   **teaspoon salt**

½   **cup granulated sugar**

½   **cup molasses**

1   **large egg**

1   **teaspoon finely grated fresh ginger**

¼   **cup finely chopped crystallized ginger**

½   **cup coarse sugar**

**1** Preheat the oven to 350°F. Lightly butter 2 baking sheets. Mix the flour, baking soda, ground ginger and salt in a medium bowl with a whisk.

**2** In a large bowl, beat the butter and granulated sugar with a mixer on medium-high speed until light and fluffy, about 5 minutes. Beat in the molasses, egg and fresh ginger. (The mixture may look curdled.) Reduce the mixer speed to low and beat in the flour mixture until combined. Stir in the crystallized ginger with a rubber spatula. The dough should be soft but not sticky; if it's sticky, refrigerate 15 minutes.

**3** Roll tablespoonfuls of dough into balls and roll in the coarse sugar. Place about 2 inches apart on the baking sheets. Bake until the cookies are set around the edges but the centers are still soft, 12 to 14 minutes. Remove the pans from the oven with oven mitts. Let the cookies cool 5 minutes on the pans, then use a spatula to move the cookies to racks to cool completely.

# PB Oatmeal-Chocolate Chip Cookies

ACTIVE: **30 min**    TOTAL: **1 hr 5 min (plus cooling)**    MAKES: **about 24**

1    cup old-fashioned rolled oats

1¼  cups all-purpose flour

½    teaspoon baking soda

½    teaspoon salt

1    stick unsalted butter,
     at room temperature

½    cup packed light brown sugar

½    cup granulated sugar

1    cup creamy peanut butter

2    large eggs

1    teaspoon pure vanilla extract

2    cups semisweet chocolate
     chips

**1** Preheat the oven to 350°F. Spread the oats on a baking sheet and bake, carefully stirring the oats occasionally with a wooden spoon, until lightly browned and toasted, 8 to 10 minutes. Remove the pan from the oven with oven mitts and let the oats cool completely.

**2** Mix the flour, baking soda and salt in a small bowl with a whisk. Beat the butter, brown sugar and granulated sugar in a large bowl with a mixer on medium-high speed until light and fluffy, about 3 minutes. Beat in the peanut butter until smooth, then beat in the eggs and vanilla. Reduce the mixer speed to low and beat in the flour mixture until combined. Stir in the oats and 1½ cups chocolate chips with a wooden spoon.

**3** Line 2 baking sheets with parchment paper. Scoop mounds of dough (about 2 tablespoons each) 1½ inches apart onto the baking sheets. Flatten with your fingers. Bake until the edges of the cookies are set but the centers are still soft, about 18 minutes. Remove the pans from the oven with oven mitts. Let the cookies cool 5 minutes on the pans, then use a spatula to move the cookies to racks to cool completely.

**4** Put the remaining ½ cup chocolate chips in a microwave-safe bowl. Microwave 30 seconds at a time, stirring, until smooth. Drizzle on the cookies using a fork. Let set 15 minutes.

## Did You Know?

Chocolate chips are engineered to withstand heat, which is why they keep their shape in cookies. If you chop up a chocolate bar, the pieces will melt and lose their shape in the oven.

# Sugar Cookies with Royal Icing

ACTIVE: **45 min**    TOTAL: **3 hr 45 min (plus cooling)**    MAKES: **24 to 36**

## FOR THE COOKIES

- 2½ cups cake flour, plus more for dusting
- 1 teaspoon baking powder
- ¼ teaspoon salt
- 2 sticks unsalted butter, at room temperature
- ¾ cup granulated sugar
- 1 large egg
- 1 teaspoon pure vanilla extract

## FOR THE ICING

- 1 1-pound box confectioners' sugar (about 3¾ cups)
- 2 tablespoons meringue powder
- 6 tablespoons water
- Nonpareils, for topping

1 Make the cookies: Mix the flour, baking powder and salt in a medium bowl with a whisk. In a large bowl, beat the butter and granulated sugar with a mixer on medium-high speed until light and fluffy, 3 to 5 minutes. Beat in the egg and vanilla. Reduce the mixer speed to low; add the flour mixture in two batches and beat until just combined. Divide the dough in half, wrap in plastic wrap and refrigerate until firm, at least 1 hour and up to 1 day.

2 Line 2 baking sheets with parchment paper. Lightly dust 1 piece of dough with flour and place between 2 pieces of parchment paper. Roll out with a rolling pin until about ⅛ inch thick. Refrigerate until slightly firm, about 15 minutes. Repeat with the other piece of dough. Cut the dough into rounds or other shapes using 2- to 4-inch cookie cutters. Place on the baking sheets. Gather the scraps and refrigerate until firm; reroll once to cut out more cookies. Refrigerate the cutouts until firm, about 30 minutes.

3 Preheat the oven to 350°F. Bake the cookies until just golden, 13 to 15 minutes. Remove the pans from the oven with oven mitts. Let the cookies cool 5 minutes on the pans, then use a spatula to move the cookies to racks to cool completely.

4 Meanwhile, make the icing: Combine the confectioners' sugar and meringue powder in a large bowl. Beat in the water with a mixer on medium speed until glossy peaks form. Spread the icing on the cookies and sprinkle with nonpareils. Let set, at least 1 hour or overnight.

# PB&J Sandwich Cookies

ACTIVE: **1 hr**    TOTAL: **2 hr 15 min (plus cooling)**    MAKES: **about 32**

1    cup all-purpose flour

½    cup whole-wheat flour

½    teaspoon baking powder

½    teaspoon kosher salt

1    stick unsalted butter,
     at room temperature

½    cup granulated sugar

½    cup packed light brown sugar

1    teaspoon pure vanilla extract

1    large egg

1½   cups creamy peanut butter

⅔    cup grape jelly

## Tip
Roll out cookie dough between two sheets of parchment paper, so you don't have to worry about it sticking to the counter!

**1** Mix the all-purpose flour, whole-wheat flour, baking powder and salt in a medium bowl with a whisk. In a large bowl, beat the butter, granulated sugar, brown sugar and vanilla with a mixer on medium-high speed until light and fluffy, about 5 minutes. Beat in the egg until combined, then beat in the peanut butter until smooth. Reduce the mixer speed to low and beat in the flour mixture until just combined.

**2** Using a rubber spatula, scrape the dough onto a piece of parchment paper and pat into a rectangle. Top with another piece of parchment and roll out the dough with a rolling pin into a ¼-inch-thick rectangle. Refrigerate until firm, about 1 hour.

**3** Preheat the oven to 375°F. Trim the edges of the dough and cut the dough into 1½-inch squares. Place the squares 2 inches apart on 2 unlined baking sheets; press each with the back of a fork to make a crisscross pattern. Gather the scraps and refrigerate until firm, if needed; reroll to cut out more cookies.

**4** Bake until the cookies are almost set, about 14 minutes. Remove the pans from the oven with oven mitts. Let the cookies cool 5 minutes on the pans, then use a spatula to move the cookies to racks to cool completely. Using a small spoon, sandwich the grape jelly (1 teaspoon per sandwich) between the cookies.

# Whoopie Pies

**Tip**

When you're making sandwich cookies like these whoopie pies, try to make all the cookies the same size—that way they'll match up when you sandwich them!

## ① Bake the Cookies

• Mix 2 cups flour, ⅔ cup unsweetened cocoa powder and 1 teaspoon each baking soda and salt in a medium bowl with a whisk. In a large bowl, beat 10 tablespoons softened butter, 1¼ cups light brown sugar and ½ teaspoon vanilla with a mixer on medium-high speed until fluffy; beat in 1 egg. On low speed, beat the flour mixture into the butter mixture in three batches, alternating with 1 cup buttermilk in two batches.

• Line 3 baking sheets with parchment paper and coat with cooking spray. Scoop 16 mounds of batter (2 tablespoons batter per cookie) onto the pans, about 2 inches apart; gently form into rounds with damp fingers and smooth the tops. Refrigerate until firm, about 30 minutes.

• Preheat the oven to 400°F. Bake the cookies until they spring back when gently pressed, 10 to 12 minutes. Remove from the oven with oven mitts. Let the cookies cool 5 minutes on the pans, then use a spatula to move the cookies to a rack to cool completely.

## ② Make Your Filling

Beat 1 stick softened butter in a large bowl with a mixer on medium speed until fluffy; gradually beat in 1 cup confectioners' sugar. Gradually beat in 2 tablespoons milk, then another 1 cup confectioners' sugar. Beat until smooth. Mix in ½ teaspoon vanilla. Pick a flavor and stir in one of the following ingredients (or leave the filling plain).

**BERRY**
• 2 tablespoons seedless raspberry jam

**CHOCOLATE**
• 2 tablespoons cocoa powder dissolved in 2 tablespoons hot water

**LEMON**
• 2½ tablespoons lemon curd

**CARAMEL**
• ¼ cup dulce de leche or thick caramel sauce

## ③ Assemble the Whoopie Pies

Sandwich about 2 tablespoons filling between 2 cookies. Repeat with the remaining cookies and filling. Roll the edges in any of the following.

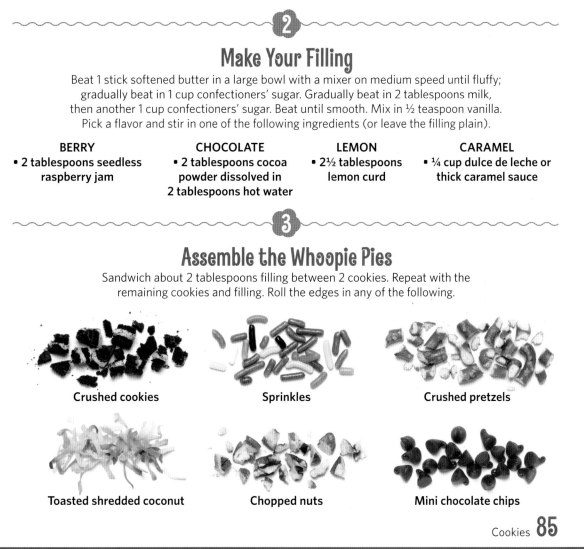

Crushed cookies

Sprinkles

Crushed pretzels

Toasted shredded coconut

Chopped nuts

Mini chocolate chips

**Tip**
A beaten egg works
like glue for pie crusts:
It can seal them
together or you can use egg
to stick toppings on dough
before baking.

# Plum Pie Cookies

ACTIVE: **1 hr**    TOTAL: **2½ hr (plus cooling)**    MAKES: **about 18**

2½ cups plus 1 tablespoon all-purpose flour

1 cup granulated sugar

¾ teaspoon salt

2 sticks unsalted butter, cut into cubes, at room temperature

1 large egg, lightly beaten, plus 1 beaten egg for brushing

½ teaspoon ground cinnamon

2 small plums

Coarse sugar, for sprinkling

**1** Pulse 2½ cups flour, ½ cup granulated sugar and the salt in a food processor until combined. Add the butter and pulse until the mixture looks crumbly. Drizzle in 1 beaten egg and pulse until the dough holds together when pinched. Scrape the dough onto a clean surface and knead a few times with your hands until the dough comes together. Divide the dough into 2 balls and place each ball on a separate piece of parchment paper. Top each with another piece of parchment and roll out with a rolling pin into an 11- to 12-inch round (about ⅛ inch thick). Refrigerate until firm, about 1 hour.

**2** Preheat the oven to 375°F. Line 2 baking sheets with parchment paper. Whisk the remaining ½ cup granulated sugar, 1 tablespoon flour and the cinnamon in a medium bowl. Halve, pit and thinly slice the plums, then cut each slice in half crosswise.

**3** Using a 2½-inch round cookie cutter, cut out small rounds as close together as possible from 1 piece of dough. Gather the scraps and refrigerate until firm; reroll once to cut out more rounds. Place 9 rounds on one of the baking sheets and brush the edges with some of the remaining beaten egg. Toss the plums in the cinnamon sugar mixture to coat, then arrange about 4 plum pieces in the center of each dough round on the pan, leaving space around the edges. Top each with a second round of dough and press the edges to seal. (If the dough is too stiff to work with, warm it briefly between your hands.) Press around the edges with a fork to seal. Cut 4 small slits in the top of each cookie with a knife. Put the cookies in the freezer and repeat with the remaining dough and plums.

**4** Lightly brush the cookies with the remaining beaten egg and sprinkle with coarse sugar. Bake until the cookies are golden brown, 22 to 25 minutes. Remove the pans from the oven with oven mitts. Let the cookies cool completely on the pans.

## Did You Know?

There's a reason fruit pies have slits on top: Steam can build up inside the pie, and if it doesn't have a way to escape, it can make the crust soggy.

# Red Velvet Crackle Cookies

ACTIVE: **45 min**     TOTAL: **3 hr (plus cooling)**     MAKES: **about 24**

- 2   ounces white chocolate, chopped
- 1¼ cups all-purpose flour
- 2   tablespoons unsweetened cocoa powder
- 1   teaspoon baking powder
- ¼   teaspoon salt
- 2   large eggs
- 3   tablespoons vegetable oil
- 1½ teaspoons red liquid food coloring
- ¾   cup granulated sugar
- 1   cup confectioners' sugar

**Tip**

Don't be alarmed: These cookies will be all white when they go in the oven. The red color will start showing once they spread.

**1** Put the white chocolate in a microwave-safe bowl and microwave 30 seconds at a time, stirring, until melted. Mix the flour, cocoa powder, baking powder and salt in a medium bowl with a whisk.

**2** In a large bowl, whisk the eggs, vegetable oil and food coloring until combined. Whisk in the granulated sugar and melted white chocolate until smooth. Stir the flour mixture into the egg mixture with a wooden spoon until combined. Scrape the dough onto a piece of plastic wrap and pat into a rectangle; tightly wrap and refrigerate until firm, at least 2 hours or overnight.

**3** Preheat the oven to 300°F. Line 2 baking sheets with parchment paper. Put the confectioners' sugar in a small bowl. Roll tablespoonfuls of dough into balls. Toss the balls in the confectioners' sugar to coat. Slightly flatten the balls, then dip again in the confectioners' sugar. Place the cookies 2 inches apart on the baking sheets.

**4** Bake until the cookies are puffed, cracked and firm, 16 to 18 minutes. Remove the pans from the oven with oven mitts. Let the cookies cool completely on the pans.

# Lime Crackle Cookies

ACTIVE: **30 min**    TOTAL: **1 hr 40 min (plus cooling)**    MAKES: **about 36**

**2½ cups all-purpose flour**

**1 teaspoon baking powder**

**½ teaspoon salt**

**1 stick unsalted butter, at room temperature**

**1¼ cups granulated sugar**

**2 large eggs**

**1 teaspoon grated lime zest, plus 1½ tablespoons lime juice**

**1½ tablespoons lemon juice**

**4 drops green liquid food coloring**

**½ cup confectioners' sugar**

**2 tablespoons green sanding sugar**

**1** Mix the flour, baking powder and salt in a medium bowl with a whisk. In a large bowl, beat the butter and granulated sugar with a mixer on medium speed until light and fluffy, about 3 minutes. Add the eggs, one at a time, beating well after each addition. Beat in the lime zest, lime juice and lemon juice, then beat in the food coloring. Reduce the mixer speed to low and gradually add the flour mixture, beating until just combined. Cover the bowl with plastic wrap and refrigerate the dough until firm, about 45 minutes.

**2** Preheat the oven to 350°F. Line 2 baking sheets with parchment paper. Combine the confectioners' sugar and sanding sugar in a small bowl. Roll tablespoonfuls of dough into balls and toss in the sugar mixture to coat. Place the cookies 2 inches apart on the baking sheets.

**3** Bake until the cookies are puffed and cracked on top and golden around the edges, 18 to 20 minutes. Remove the pans from the oven with oven mitts. Let the cookies cool 5 minutes on the pans, then use a spatula to move the cookies to racks to cool completely.

# Rainbow Slice-and-Bake Cookies

ACTIVE: **1 hr**    TOTAL: **2½ hr (plus cooling)**    MAKES: **about 36**

2½ cups all-purpose flour,
   plus more for dusting

½   teaspoon baking powder

¼   teaspoon salt

2   sticks unsalted butter,
    at room temperature

¾   cup granulated sugar

¾   cup confectioners' sugar

2   large egg yolks

2   teaspoons pure
    vanilla extract

¼   teaspoon each red, orange,
    yellow, green, blue and
    purple gel food coloring

1   cup white candy melts

## Tip
You'll need a lot of food coloring for this recipe—and it can get messy. Wear latex gloves so you don't accidentally end up with rainbow hands!

**1** Mix the flour, baking powder and salt in a medium bowl with a whisk. In a large bowl, beat the butter, granulated sugar and confectioners' sugar with a mixer on medium-high speed until light and fluffy, about 2 minutes. Beat in the egg yolks and vanilla until smooth. Reduce the mixer speed to medium low and gradually beat in the flour mixture until the dough just comes together.

**2** Divide the dough into 6 pieces: 2 large pieces (about 7 ounces each), 2 medium pieces (about 5 ounces each) and 2 small pieces (about 3 ounces each). Tint 1 large piece of dough red and the other orange, kneading the food coloring into the dough with gloved hands or a rubber spatula. Tint 1 medium piece of dough yellow and the other green. Tint 1 small piece of dough blue and the other purple.

**3** Using gloved hands, roll the purple dough into a 7-inch log (about ¾ inch thick) on a floured sheet of parchment. Using a rolling pin, roll out the remaining pieces of dough into rectangles on separate floured sheets of parchment, dusting with more flour as needed: 3½ by 7 inches for blue; 5 by 7½ inches for green; 6 by 8 inches for yellow; 7 by 8½ inches for orange; 8 by 9 inches for red.

**4** Tightly wrap the blue dough around the purple log, keeping the dough in a log shape; pinch the seam to close. Continue wrapping the log with the dough: next green, yellow, orange and red. Wrap the whole log in plastic wrap; freeze until very firm, about 1 hour.

**5** Preheat the oven to 375°F. Trim the ends of the dough log, then slice the log into ⅜-inch-thick rounds. Slice each round in half. Place the cookies about 1 inch apart on 2 unlined baking sheets and refrigerate until firm, at least 15 minutes.

**6** Bake one pan at a time until the cookies are set around the edges and golden on the bottom, 10 to 15 minutes. Remove the pans from the oven with oven mitts. Let the cookies cool 5 minutes on the pans, then use a spatula to move the cookies to racks to cool completely.

**7** Meanwhile, put the candy melts in a medium microwave-safe bowl and microwave 30 seconds at a time, stirring, until smooth, about 2 minutes. Pour into a resealable plastic bag and snip a corner. Pipe small clouds on the ends of each rainbow. Let set, at least 5 minutes.

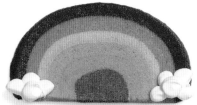

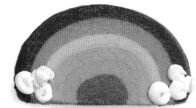

# Gluten-Free Coconut Snowballs

ACTIVE: **25 min**    TOTAL: **2 hr (plus cooling)**    MAKES: **about 18**

1½ cups rice flour

½ cup unsweetened finely shredded coconut

1¼ sticks (10 tablespoons) unsalted butter, at room temperature

1¼ cups confectioners' sugar

Pinch of salt

1 vanilla bean, split lengthwise and seeds scraped out

1 large egg

**1** Mix the rice flour and coconut in a small bowl with a whisk. In a large bowl, beat the butter, ½ cup confectioners' sugar, the salt and vanilla seeds with a mixer on medium speed until smooth and creamy, about 2 minutes. Beat the egg into the butter mixture, then beat in the flour mixture until just combined. Cover the dough with plastic wrap and refrigerate until it is no longer sticky, about 1 hour.

**2** Preheat the oven to 325°F. Roll heaping tablespoonfuls of dough into balls and place 1 inch apart on an unlined baking sheet. Refrigerate until firm, about 15 minutes.

**3** Bake until the cookies are set and lightly browned on the bottom, about 20 minutes. Remove the pan from the oven with oven mitts. Let the cookies cool 10 minutes on the pan.

**4** Put the remaining ¾ cup confectioners' sugar in a small bowl. Gently roll the warm cookies in the confectioners' sugar and return to the pan. Reroll the cookies in the confectioners' sugar, then place on a rack to cool completely.

## Tip

This recipe calls for rice flour (which is naturally gluten-free) in place of all-purpose flour. Be sure to check the label: Some products are processed in a place that also processes wheat.

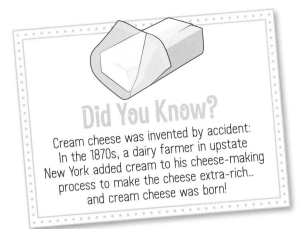

# Milk Chocolate Cookie Cups

ACTIVE: **35 min**    TOTAL: **2 hr 35 min (plus cooling)**    MAKES: **24**

**1** stick unsalted butter, at room temperature

**2** ounces cream cheese, at room temperature

**½** cup packed light brown sugar

**¼** cup granulated sugar

**¼** teaspoon salt

**1** large egg

**1** teaspoon pure vanilla extract

**1¼** cups all-purpose flour

**8** ounces milk chocolate, finely chopped

**Cooking spray**

**3 to 4** tablespoons heavy cream

**M&M's, for topping**

**1** Beat the butter, cream cheese, brown sugar, granulated sugar and salt in a medium bowl with a mixer on medium speed until smooth and creamy, about 2 minutes. Beat in the egg and vanilla until combined. Reduce the mixer speed to low and beat in the flour until combined. Beat in about one-quarter of the chopped chocolate. Cover the bowl with plastic wrap and refrigerate until the dough is no longer sticky, about 1 hour.

**2** Coat a 24-cup mini-muffin pan with cooking spray. Divide the dough among the cups (about 1 heaping tablespoon each); press into the bottoms and up the sides to create cups. (If the dough becomes sticky, dampen your fingers.) Refrigerate until firm, about 30 minutes.

**3** Preheat the oven to 350°F. Bake the cookie cups until browned around the edges and dry in the centers, 15 to 20 minutes. Remove the pan from the oven with oven mitts. Let the cookies cool 5 minutes in the pan. Use the back of a small spoon to gently indent the center of each. Use an offset spatula to remove the cookies from the pan and move to a rack to cool completely.

**4** Meanwhile, put the remaining chopped chocolate and 3 tablespoons heavy cream in a microwave-safe bowl. Microwave 30 seconds at a time, stirring, until smooth. Let stand until thick like hot fudge, about 10 minutes. (If the chocolate is too thick, gradually stir in 1 more tablespoon heavy cream. If the chocolate hardens, return it to the microwave.) Spoon the chocolate into the cookies and top with the M&M's. Let cool completely.

## Tip

To get this picture-perfect spiral, be sure to roll out the yellow and white dough to the same thickness. And when you roll them up, keep the log nice and tight.

# Lemonade Pinwheels

ACTIVE: **1 hr**   TOTAL: **6 hr 15 min (plus cooling)**   MAKES: **about 36**

- **2** cups all-purpose flour, plus more for dusting
- **½** teaspoon salt
- **½** teaspoon baking powder
- **¼** teaspoon baking soda
- **1½** sticks (12 tablespoons) unsalted butter, at room temperature
- **⅔** cup granulated sugar
- **1** large egg
- **½** teaspoon pure vanilla extract
- **¼** teaspoon pure lemon extract
- **¼** cup lemon gelatin powder (from one 3-ounce box)
- **2** tablespoons grated lemon zest (from 2 lemons), plus 1 teaspoon lemon juice
- **½** teaspoon yellow gel food coloring
- **2** tablespoons yellow sanding sugar
- **1** tablespoon coarse white sugar

**1** Mix the flour, salt, baking powder and baking soda in a medium bowl with a whisk. In a large bowl, beat the butter and granulated sugar with a mixer on medium-high speed until light and fluffy, 3 to 5 minutes. Beat in the egg, then the vanilla and lemon extracts. Reduce the mixer speed to low and beat in the flour mixture until just combined.

**2** Remove half the dough to a large piece of plastic wrap, flatten into a disk and wrap. Add 2 tablespoons gelatin powder, the lemon zest and juice and the yellow gel food coloring to the remaining dough and beat with the mixer until combined. Scrape out onto another piece of plastic wrap, flatten into a disk and wrap. Refrigerate both disks until firm, at least 2 hours or overnight.

**3** Roll out each disk of dough with a rolling pin into a 10-by-11-inch rectangle on a lightly floured surface. Put the plain dough on top of the yellow dough and trim the edges with a sharp knife. Sprinkle 1 tablespoon yellow sanding sugar over the top of the dough and gently spread to evenly cover. Starting with a long end, roll up the dough into a tight log. Wrap in plastic wrap and refrigerate until firm, at least 3 hours or overnight.

**4** Preheat the oven to 350°F. Line 2 baking sheets with parchment paper. Mix the remaining 2 tablespoons gelatin powder, 1 tablespoon yellow sanding sugar and the coarse white sugar in a small bowl; sprinkle on a sheet of parchment. Roll the dough log in the sugar mixture, pressing to adhere. Using a sharp knife, slice the log into ⅜-inch-thick rounds. Place 1½ inches apart on the baking sheets.

**5** Bake until set around the edges, about 15 minutes. Remove the pans from the oven with oven mitts. Let the cookies cool 5 minutes on the pans, then use a spatula to move the cookies to racks to cool completely.

## Did You Know?
Lemonade is older than you might think. Sources say the earliest written record of the drink goes all the way back to the year 1000 in Egypt!

# Cookie Puzzle

Turn ordinary sugar cookie dough into an edible jigsaw puzzle!

## How to Make a Cookie Puzzle

**1** Follow the recipe for the sugar cookie dough on page 82. Divide the dough in half and refrigerate as directed.

**2** Preheat the oven to 350°F. Roll out 1 piece of dough on a floured piece of parchment paper into a rectangle (about 7 by 11 inches). Trim the edges with a knife to make them straight.

**3** Slide the dough and parchment onto a baking sheet. Bake until golden, 12 to 15 minutes.

**4** Remove the pan from the oven with oven mitts. While the cookie is still warm, carefully cut in half crosswise, then cut each half into 4 puzzle pieces with a paring knife. Let cool completely on the pan, then recut the puzzle pieces and carefully separate. Repeat with the other piece of dough.

**5** To decorate, mix ½ cup confectioners' sugar and 1 to 2 tablespoons water in a small bowl with a spoon. Spread the icing on the cookies. Sprinkle with colored sanding sugar.

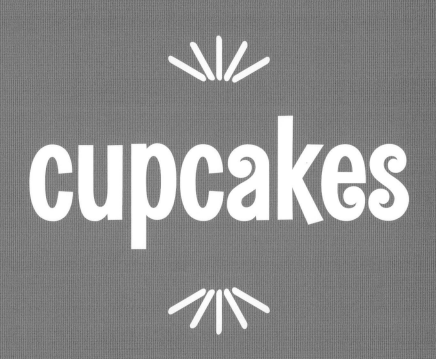

# cupcakes

# Classic Vanilla Cupcakes

ACTIVE: **40 min**    TOTAL: **1 hr (plus cooling)**    MAKES: **12**

**FOR THE CUPCAKES**

1⅓ cups all-purpose flour

1 teaspoon baking powder

½ teaspoon salt

1 stick unsalted butter, at room temperature

1 cup granulated sugar

2 large eggs

2 teaspoons pure vanilla extract

½ cup milk

**FOR THE FROSTING**

4 tablespoons unsalted butter, at room temperature

6 ounces cream cheese, at room temperature

1 teaspoon pure vanilla extract

Pinch of salt

2 cups confectioners' sugar

Rainbow nonpareils, for topping

1 Make the cupcakes: Preheat the oven to 350˚F. Line a 12-cup muffin pan with paper liners. Mix the flour, baking powder and salt in a medium bowl with a whisk.

2 In a large bowl, beat the butter with a mixer on medium-high speed until smooth, about 1 minute. Add the granulated sugar and beat until creamy, about 4 more minutes. Beat in the eggs, one at a time, then the vanilla. With the mixer on low speed, beat in the flour mixture in three batches, alternating with the milk in two batches. Increase the speed to medium high and beat until just combined.

3 Spoon the batter into the muffin cups, filling each three-quarters of the way. Bake until the tops of the cupcakes spring back when pressed gently, 20 to 25 minutes. Remove the pan from the oven with oven mitts. Let the cupcakes cool 5 minutes in the pan, then remove from the pan and let cool completely on a rack.

4 Meanwhile, make the frosting: Put the butter, cream cheese, vanilla and salt in a large bowl and beat with a mixer on medium speed until creamy, 1 to 2 minutes. Gradually beat in the confectioners' sugar on medium-low speed until smooth, then beat on medium high until thick and fluffy, 1 to 2 more minutes.

5 Spoon the frosting into a piping bag or resealable plastic bag, snip a corner and pipe the frosting on the cupcakes (or spread the frosting on top). Sprinkle with nonpareils.

## Tip
To make this pretty swirl of frosting, hold your piping bag perpendicular to the cupcake and pipe a spiral, starting from the outer edge of the cupcake and working your way to the middle.

# Gluten-Free Vanilla Cupcakes

ACTIVE: **40 min**   TOTAL: **1 hr (plus cooling)**   MAKES: **12**

## FOR THE CUPCAKES

- **1 cup brown rice flour**
- **⅓ cup tapioca flour**
- **1 teaspoon baking powder**
- **½ teaspoon salt**
- **1 stick unsalted butter, at room temperature**
- **1 cup granulated sugar**
- **2 large eggs**
- **2 teaspoons pure vanilla extract**
- **½ cup milk**

## FOR THE FROSTING

- **1½ sticks (12 tablespoons) unsalted butter, at room temperature**
- **3 cups confectioners' sugar**
- **Pinch of salt**
- **2 teaspoons pure vanilla extract**
- **2 tablespoons milk**
- **Sanding sugar, for topping**

**1** Make the cupcakes: Preheat the oven to 350°F. Line a 12-cup muffin pan with paper liners. Mix the brown rice flour, tapioca flour, baking powder and salt in a medium bowl with a whisk.

**2** Put the butter in a large bowl and beat with a mixer on medium-high speed until smooth, about 1 minute. Add the granulated sugar and beat until creamy, about 4 minutes. Beat in the eggs, one at a time, then the vanilla. With the mixer on low speed, beat in the flour mixture in three batches, alternating with the milk in two batches. Increase the speed to medium high and beat until just combined.

**3** Spoon the batter into the muffin cups, filling each three-quarters of the way. Bake until the tops of the cupcakes spring back when pressed gently, 20 to 25 minutes. Remove the pan from the oven with oven mitts. Let the cupcakes cool 5 minutes in the pan, then remove from the pan and let cool completely on a rack.

**4** Meanwhile, make the frosting: Put the butter, confectioners' sugar and salt in a large bowl and beat with a mixer on medium speed until just combined. Add the vanilla and beat on medium-high speed until creamy, about 3 minutes. Add the milk and beat until fluffy, about 1 more minute.

**5** Spread the frosting on the cupcakes and sprinkle with sanding sugar.

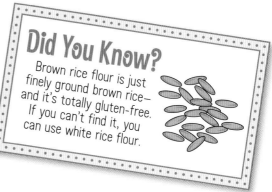

### Did You Know?

Brown rice flour is just finely ground brown rice—and it's totally gluten-free. If you can't find it, you can use white rice flour.

# Jelly Doughnut Cupcakes

ACTIVE: **40 min**    TOTAL: **1 hr (plus cooling)**    MAKES: **12**

**FOR THE CUPCAKES**

1⅓ cups all-purpose flour

1 teaspoon baking powder

½ teaspoon salt

1 stick unsalted butter, at room temperature

1 cup granulated sugar

2 large eggs

2 teaspoons pure vanilla extract

½ cup milk

**FOR THE FROSTING AND FILLING**

1½ sticks (12 tablespoons) unsalted butter, at room temperature

3 cups confectioners' sugar

Pinch of salt

2 teaspoons pure vanilla extract

2 tablespoons milk

½ cup seedless raspberry jam

Sanding sugar, for sprinkling

1 Make the cupcakes: Preheat the oven to 350°F. Line a 12-cup muffin pan with paper liners. Mix the flour, baking powder and salt in a medium bowl with a whisk.

2 Beat the butter in a large bowl with a mixer on medium-high speed until smooth, about 1 minute. Add the granulated sugar and beat until creamy, about 4 more minutes. Beat in the eggs, one at a time, then the vanilla. With the mixer on low speed, beat in the flour mixture in three batches, alternating with the milk in two batches. Increase the speed to medium high and beat until just combined.

3 Spoon the batter into the muffin cups, filling each three-quarters of the way. Bake until the tops of the cupcakes spring back when pressed gently, 20 to 25 minutes. Remove the pan from the oven with oven mitts. Let the cupcakes cool 5 minutes in the pan, then remove from the pan and let cool completely on a rack.

4 Meanwhile, make the frosting: Put the butter, confectioners' sugar and salt in a large bowl and beat with a mixer on medium speed until just combined. Add the vanilla and beat on medium-high speed until creamy, about 3 minutes. Beat in the milk until fluffy, about 1 more minute.

5 Spoon the jam into a piping bag with a large round tip. Insert the tip into the tops of each cupcake and pipe in the jam. Spread the frosting on the cupcakes and sprinkle with sanding sugar.

# Blueberry-Maple Cupcakes

ACTIVE: **40 min**    TOTAL: **1 hr (plus cooling)**    MAKES: **12**

## FOR THE CUPCAKES

1⅓ cups all-purpose flour

1 teaspoon baking powder

½ teaspoon salt

1 stick unsalted butter, at room temperature

1 cup granulated sugar

2 large eggs

2 teaspoons pure vanilla extract

½ teaspoon maple extract

½ cup milk

## FOR THE FROSTING

1½ sticks (12 tablespoons) unsalted butter, at room temperature

3 cups confectioners' sugar

Pinch of salt

2 teaspoons pure vanilla extract

1 teaspoon grated lemon zest

2 tablespoons milk

½ cup blueberries

Pure maple syrup, for drizzling

1 Make the cupcakes: Preheat the oven to 350˚F. Line a 12-cup muffin pan with paper liners. Mix the flour, baking powder and salt in a medium bowl with a whisk.

2 Beat the butter in a large bowl with a mixer on medium-high speed until smooth, about 1 minute. Add the granulated sugar and beat until creamy, about 4 more minutes. Beat in the eggs, one at a time, then the vanilla and maple extracts. With the mixer on low speed, beat in the flour mixture in three batches, alternating with the milk in two batches. Increase the speed to medium high and beat until just combined.

3 Spoon the batter into the muffin cups, filling each three-quarters of the way. Bake until the tops of the cupcakes spring back when pressed gently, 20 to 25 minutes. Remove the pan from the oven with oven mitts. Let the cupcakes cool 5 minutes in the pan, then remove from the pan and let cool completely on a rack.

4 Meanwhile, make the frosting: Put the butter, confectioners' sugar and salt in a large bowl and beat with a mixer on medium speed until just combined. Add the vanilla and lemon zest and beat on medium-high speed until creamy, about 3 minutes. Beat in the milk until fluffy, about 1 more minute.

5 Spread the frosting on the cupcakes. Toss the blueberries with a drizzle of maple syrup in a small bowl. Top each cupcake with a few blueberries.

### Did You Know?

Pure maple syrup is made from the sap of maple trees. Pancake syrup doesn't come from trees at all—it's usually made from corn syrup.

# Cinnamon Dulce de Leche Cupcakes

ACTIVE: **40 min**  TOTAL: **1 hr (plus cooling)**  MAKES: **12**

## FOR THE CUPCAKES

1¼ cups all-purpose flour

½ teaspoon baking powder

½ teaspoon baking soda

½ teaspoon salt

1 teaspoon ground cinnamon

1 stick unsalted butter, melted

½ cup granulated sugar

½ cup packed light brown sugar

½ cup sour cream

2 large eggs

1 teaspoon pure vanilla extract

## FOR THE FROSTING

4 tablespoons unsalted butter, at room temperature

6 ounces cream cheese, at room temperature

1 teaspoon pure vanilla extract

Pinch of salt

1 cup dulce de leche, plus more for topping

1 Make the cupcakes: Preheat the oven to 350°F. Line a 12-cup muffin pan with paper liners. Mix the flour, baking powder, baking soda, salt and cinnamon in a medium bowl with a whisk.

2 Whisk the melted butter, granulated sugar, brown sugar, sour cream, eggs and vanilla in a large bowl until smooth. Whisk in the flour mixture until just combined.

3 Spoon the batter into the muffin cups, filling each three-quarters of the way. Bake until the tops of the cupcakes spring back when pressed gently, 18 to 20 minutes. Remove the pan from the oven with oven mitts. Let the cupcakes cool 5 minutes in the pan, then remove from the pan and let cool completely on a rack.

4 Meanwhile, make the frosting: Beat the butter, cream cheese, vanilla and salt in a large bowl with a mixer on medium speed until creamy, 1 to 2 minutes. Gradually beat in the dulce de leche on medium-low speed until smooth, then beat on medium high until thick and fluffy, 1 to 2 more minutes.

5 Spread the frosting on the cupcakes and top each cupcake with a spoonful of dulce de leche.

# Cookies-and-Cream Cupcakes

ACTIVE: 45 min    TOTAL: 1 hr 5 min (plus cooling)    MAKES: 12

## FOR THE CUPCAKES

- ⅔ cup refrigerated chocolate chip cookie dough
- 1¼ cups all-purpose flour
- 1 teaspoon baking powder
- ½ teaspoon salt
- 1 stick unsalted butter, at room temperature
- 1 cup granulated sugar
- 2 large eggs
- 2 teaspoons pure vanilla extract
- ½ cup milk

## FOR THE FROSTING

- 1½ sticks (12 tablespoons) unsalted butter, at room temperature
- 3 cups confectioners' sugar
- Pinch of salt
- 2 teaspoons pure vanilla extract
- 2 tablespoons milk
- ⅔ cup crushed chocolate sandwich cookies (6 cookies), plus broken pieces for topping

1 Make the cupcakes: Preheat the oven to 350°F. Line a 12-cup muffin pan with paper liners. Roll the cookie dough with your fingers into 12 small balls.

2 Mix the flour, baking powder and salt in a medium bowl with a whisk. Beat the butter in a large bowl with a mixer on medium-high speed until smooth, about 1 minute. Beat in the granulated sugar until creamy, about 4 minutes. Beat in the eggs, one at a time, then the vanilla. With the mixer on low speed, beat in the flour mixture in three batches, alternating with the milk in two batches. Increase the speed to medium high and beat until just combined.

3 Spoon the batter into the muffin cups, filling each three-quarters of the way. Top each cupcake with a cookie dough ball. Bake until the tops of the cupcakes spring back when pressed gently, 20 to 25 minutes. Remove the pan from the oven with oven mitts. Let the cupcakes cool 5 minutes in the pan, then remove from the pan and let cool completely on a rack.

4 Meanwhile, make the frosting: Beat the butter, confectioners' sugar and salt in a large bowl with a mixer on medium speed until just combined. Add the vanilla and beat on medium-high speed until creamy, about 3 minutes. Beat in the milk until fluffy, about 1 minute. Fold in the crushed sandwich cookies.

5 Spread the frosting on the cupcakes and top with broken sandwich cookies.

**Tip**
This frosting has crushed cookies in it, so it's not great for piping. Spread the frosting instead, then add a piece of a cookie to make the top look more fun.

## Tip

This frosting is a ganache, which sounds fancy but it's super easy to make. If you like your frosting less sweet, use a darker, bittersweet chocolate.

# Mini Double Chocolate Cupcakes

ACTIVE: 45 min    TOTAL: 1 hr (plus cooling)    MAKES: 24

## FOR THE CUPCAKES

- 2  ounces bittersweet chocolate, finely chopped
- ¼  cup unsweetened cocoa powder
- ¼  cup packed light brown sugar
- ¼  cup hot brewed coffee or hot water
- ½  cup all-purpose flour
- ¼  cup granulated sugar
- ½  teaspoon salt
- ¼  teaspoon baking soda
- 1  large egg plus 1 egg yolk
- ¼  cup vegetable oil
- ¼  cup buttermilk
- 1  teaspoon pure vanilla extract

## FOR THE FROSTING

- 1  cup heavy cream
- 2  tablespoons light corn syrup
- 2  tablespoons unsalted butter

Pinch of salt

- 8  ounces semisweet chocolate, chopped

**1** Make the cupcakes: Preheat the oven to 325°F. Line a 24-cup mini-muffin pan with liners. Put the chocolate, cocoa powder and brown sugar in a large bowl, then mix in the hot coffee or water with a whisk. Let cool to room temperature.

**2** Combine the flour, granulated sugar, salt and baking soda in a medium bowl with a whisk. Whisk the whole egg, egg yolk, vegetable oil, buttermilk and vanilla into the melted chocolate mixture. Add the flour mixture and whisk until smooth.

**3** Spoon a little less than a tablespoon of batter into each of the mini-muffin cups. Bake until a toothpick inserted into the center of a cupcake comes out clean, about 15 minutes. Remove the pan from the oven with oven mitts. Let the cupcakes cool 5 minutes in the pan, then remove from the pan and let cool completely on a rack.

**4** Meanwhile, make the frosting: Fill a large bowl halfway with ice water. Combine the heavy cream, corn syrup, butter and salt in a medium saucepan and bring to a simmer. Carefully remove from the heat, then add the chocolate and stir with a whisk until smooth. Carefully place the bowl in the ice water (don't let the water get in the chocolate mixture!). Let sit, stirring every few minutes with a spoon, until thick enough to spread, about 15 minutes.

**5** Spoon the frosting into a piping bag with a star tip and pipe onto the cupcakes (or spread the frosting on top).

### Did You Know?

Cocoa powder is made from cacao beans—and that's not a typo! The cacao beans are fermented, dried, roasted, crushed and ground before they become cocoa.

COCOA
100% CACAO
NATURAL UNSWEETENED

# Mini Chocolate Chip Cupcakes

ACTIVE: **30 min**    TOTAL: **50 min (plus cooling)**    MAKES: **36**

## FOR THE CUPCAKES

- 1⅓ cups all-purpose flour
- 1 teaspoon baking powder
- ½ teaspoon salt
- 1 stick unsalted butter, at room temperature
- 1 cup granulated sugar
- 2 large eggs
- 2 teaspoons pure vanilla extract
- ½ cup milk
- ½ cup mini chocolate chips

## FOR THE FROSTING

- 1½ sticks (12 tablespoons) unsalted butter, at room temperature
- 3 cups confectioners' sugar
- Pinch of salt
- 2 teaspoons pure vanilla extract
- 2 tablespoons milk
- Flaky sea salt and mini chocolate chips, for topping

**1** Make the cupcakes: Preheat the oven to 350°F. Line 36 mini-muffin cups with paper liners. Mix the flour, baking powder and salt in a medium bowl with a whisk.

**2** Beat the butter in a large bowl with a mixer on medium-high speed until smooth, about 1 minute. Add the granulated sugar and beat until creamy, about 4 more minutes. Beat in the eggs, one at a time, then the vanilla. With the mixer on low speed, beat in the flour mixture in three batches, alternating with the milk in two batches. Increase the speed to medium high and beat until just combined. Stir in the chocolate chips with a rubber spatula.

**3** Spoon a little less than a tablespoon of batter into each of the mini-muffin cups. Bake until the tops of the cupcakes spring back when pressed gently, about 15 minutes. Remove the pans from the oven with oven mitts. Let the cupcakes cool 5 minutes in the pans, then remove from the pans and let cool completely on a rack.

**4** Meanwhile, make the frosting: Beat the butter, confectioners' sugar and salt in a large bowl with a mixer on medium speed until just combined. Add the vanilla and beat on medium-high speed until creamy, about 3 minutes. Beat in the milk until fluffy, about 1 more minute.

**5** Spoon the frosting into a piping bag with a small star tip and pipe on the cupcakes (or spread the frosting on top). Sprinkle with flaky sea salt and mini chocolate chips.

**Did You Know?**
You can make any cupcake in mini form. If you're using a full-size cupcake recipe to make mini cupcakes, you'll end up with at least three times as many cupcakes!

# Sweet-and-Salty Cupcakes

ACTIVE: **40 min**   TOTAL: **1 hr (plus cooling)**   MAKES: **12**

## FOR THE CUPCAKES

1   cup all-purpose flour

½   teaspoon baking soda

½   teaspoon salt

¾   cup milk

½   cup unsweetened
    cocoa powder

1   cup granulated sugar

¾   cup vegetable oil

1   large egg

1   teaspoon pure vanilla extract

½   cup crushed potato chips,
    plus more for topping

½   cup crushed chocolate-
    covered pretzels,
    plus more for topping

## FOR THE FROSTING

4   ounces semisweet chocolate,
    chopped

1   stick unsalted butter,
    at room temperature

2   cups confectioners' sugar

2   tablespoons unsweetened
    cocoa powder

2   tablespoons milk

1   teaspoon pure
    vanilla extract

**1** Make the cupcakes: Preheat the oven to 350˚F. Line a 12-cup muffin pan with paper liners. Mix the flour, baking soda and salt in a medium bowl with a whisk.

**2** Heat the milk in a small saucepan over medium heat until hot but not boiling. Put the cocoa powder in a large bowl, pour in the hot milk, and whisk until smooth. Let cool slightly. Whisk in the granulated sugar, vegetable oil, egg and vanilla until smooth. Whisk in the flour mixture until just combined. Stir in the potato chips and pretzels with a rubber spatula.

**3** Spoon the batter into the muffin cups, filling each three-quarters of the way. Bake until the tops of the cupcakes spring back when pressed gently, 20 to 25 minutes. Remove the pan from the oven with oven mitts. Let the cupcakes cool 5 minutes in the pan, then remove from the pan and let cool completely on a rack.

**4** Meanwhile, make the frosting: Put the chocolate in a microwave-safe bowl and microwave, stirring every 20 seconds, until melted. Let cool. Combine the melted chocolate, butter, confectioners' sugar, cocoa powder, milk and vanilla in a food processor. Pulse until smooth.

**5** Spread the frosting on the cupcakes and top with more crushed potato chips and chocolate-covered pretzels.

## Tip
Add the potato chips and chocolate-covered pretzels at the last minute so the toppings will stay crunchy.

# Sundae Cupcakes

ACTIVE: **1 hr 20 min**    TOTAL: **2 hr (plus cooling)**    MAKES: **12**

## FOR THE CUPCAKES

1   stick unsalted butter, cut into pieces

2   ounces unsweetened chocolate, chopped

1   cup granulated sugar

2   large eggs

¾   cup all-purpose flour

¼   teaspoon baking powder

¼   teaspoon baking soda

¼   teaspoon salt

¼   cup whole milk

1   banana, chopped

¼   cup salted roasted peanuts, chopped

## FOR THE FROSTING

2½ sticks unsalted butter, at room temperature

2½ cups confectioners' sugar

Pinch of salt

1½ teaspoons pure vanilla extract

2   tablespoons whole milk

2   sugar ice cream cones, crushed

## FOR THE TOPPINGS

1   7-ounce bottle chocolate shell topping

Rainbow sprinkles, for topping

**1** Make the cupcakes: Preheat the oven to 350°F. Line a 12-cup muffin pan with paper or foil liners. Combine the butter and chocolate in a large microwave-safe bowl; microwave, stirring every 30 seconds, until melted. Let cool slightly, then mix in the granulated sugar and eggs with a whisk until smooth. Whisk in the flour, baking powder, baking soda and salt until just combined. Add the milk and whisk until smooth. Stir in the banana and peanuts with a wooden spoon.

**2** Spoon the batter into the muffin cups, filling each three-quarters of the way. Bake until the tops of the cupcakes spring back when pressed gently, about 20 minutes. Remove the pan from the oven with oven mitts. Let the cupcakes cool 5 minutes in the pan, then remove from the pan and let cool completely on a rack.

**3** Meanwhile, make the frosting: Beat the butter, confectioners' sugar and salt in a large bowl with a mixer on medium speed until combined. Add the vanilla and milk; increase the speed to medium high and beat until light and fluffy, about 3 minutes. Add the crushed sugar cones and beat 1 more minute. Spoon the frosting into a piping bag with a large star tip. Place the cupcakes on a baking sheet and pipe tall swirls of frosting onto the cupcakes. Refrigerate until the frosting is firm, about 20 minutes.

**4** Pour the chocolate shell into a short wide drinking glass. One at a time, turn each cupcake upside down and dunk the frosted tops in the chocolate; rotate to coat and let the excess drip off. Return to the baking sheet and top with sprinkles while the chocolate is still wet. Refrigerate until set, at least 30 minutes.

## Did You Know?

Chocolate shell works like magic: It hardens almost instantly when it hits something cold like ice cream or this chilled frosting. The secret ingredient is coconut oil!

# Mix Up Your
# Frosting!

Make frosting in amazing new colors—with a basic box of food coloring.

You can make these colors with a standard box of
red (r), yellow (y), blue (b) and green (g) liquid food coloring.
Mix 1 cup store-bought white frosting with the drops indicated.
Don't be alarmed: 100 drops is only about 1 teaspoon!

| | | | | | |
|---|---|---|---|---|---|
| 1r | 3r, 1y | 4r | 14r | 45r, 5y | 111r |
| 3y | 22y, 2r | 120y | 45y, 15r | 45y, 44r | 80y, 45r |
| 10g, 5y | 4b, 4y | 24y, 22b | 20y, 10g | 78g | 78g, 46b |
| 6g, 5b | 3b, 3g | 4b | 12b | 58b | 108b, 30g |
| 5b, 3r | 24r, 20b | 60r, 39b | 24r, 20b | 153r, 42b | 180r, 80b |

**Tip**

You won't find sweetened condensed milk in the dairy aisle—it's sold in cans with the baking ingredients. It's super thick and sweet.

# Milk-and-Cookies Cupcakes

ACTIVE: 1 hr     TOTAL: 1½ hr (plus cooling)     MAKES: 12

## FOR THE CUPCAKES

1   stick unsalted butter,
    at room temperature

⅔   cup plus 2 tablespoons
    sweetened condensed milk

¼   cup granulated sugar

1   large egg

1   teaspoon pure vanilla extract

½   teaspoon salt

1   cup all-purpose flour

1   teaspoon baking powder

¼   teaspoon baking soda

¼   cup plus 2 tablespoons
    whole milk

2   tablespoons mini
    chocolate chips

## FOR THE FROSTING

6   ounces milk chocolate,
    chopped

1½  sticks (12 tablespoons)
    unsalted butter,
    at room temperature

¼   cup sweetened condensed
    milk, plus more for topping

Pinch of salt

¾   cup confectioners' sugar

Mini chocolate chip cookies,
    for topping

**1** Make the cupcakes: Preheat the oven to 325°F. Line a 12-cup muffin pan with paper or foil liners. Combine the butter, ⅔ cup condensed milk, the granulated sugar, egg, vanilla and salt in a food processor. Process until smooth and slightly thickened, about 2 minutes. Add the flour, baking powder and baking soda and pulse a few times until blended. Drizzle in ¼ cup whole milk and pulse a few times until smooth.

**2** Spoon the batter into the muffin cups, filling each three-quarters of the way. Sprinkle the mini chocolate chips on top. Bake until the tops of the cupcakes are golden and spring back when pressed gently, 20 to 25 minutes. Remove the pan from the oven with oven mitts. Let the cupcakes cool 5 minutes in the pan, then remove from the pan and place on a rack.

**3** Poke the warm cupcakes all over with a toothpick. Mix the remaining 2 tablespoons each condensed milk and whole milk in a small bowl with a spoon; using a piping brush, brush the milk mixture evenly over the warm cupcakes. Let cool completely.

**4** Meanwhile, make the frosting: Put the milk chocolate in a microwave-safe bowl and microwave, stirring every 30 seconds, until smooth. Let cool slightly. Combine the melted chocolate, butter, condensed milk and salt in a food processor and process until smooth. Add the confectioners' sugar and process until smooth, about 1 more minute. Scrape into a bowl and refrigerate until firm but still spreadable, about 20 minutes.

**5** Spread the frosting on the cupcakes. Make a small well in the middle of the frosting. Fill each well with a little condensed milk. Top with mini cookies.

## Did You Know?

Chocolate chip cookies are America's favorite cookie—by a long shot! Peanut butter cookies and oatmeal cookies come in a distant 2nd and 3rd place.

# Chocolate Cheesecake Cupcakes

ACTIVE: **40 min**   TOTAL: **1 hr (plus cooling)**   MAKES: **12**

## FOR THE CUPCAKES

- ¾ cup chocolate graham cracker crumbs
- 1 stick unsalted butter, at room temperature, plus 3 tablespoons, melted
- 1⅓ cups all-purpose flour
- 1 teaspoon baking powder
- ½ teaspoon salt
- 1 cup granulated sugar
- 2 large eggs
- 2 teaspoons pure vanilla extract
- ½ cup milk

## FOR THE FROSTING

- 4 tablespoons unsalted butter, at room temperature
- 6 ounces cream cheese, at room temperature
- 1 teaspoon pure vanilla extract
- Pinch of salt
- 2 cups confectioners' sugar
- ½ cup unsweetened cocoa powder

**1** Make the cupcakes: Preheat the oven to 350˚F. Line a 12-cup muffin pan with paper liners. Combine the graham cracker crumbs and melted butter with a spoon in a small bowl. Press into the bottom of each cupcake liner using the back of the spoon, reserving a little for topping. Mix the flour, baking powder and salt in a medium bowl with a whisk.

**2** Beat the remaining 1 stick butter in a large bowl with a mixer on medium-high speed until smooth, about 1 minute. Add the granulated sugar and beat until creamy, about 4 more minutes. Beat in the eggs, one at a time, then the vanilla. With the mixer on low speed, beat in the flour mixture in three batches, alternating with the milk in two batches. Increase the speed to medium high and beat until just combined.

**3** Spoon the batter into the muffin cups, filling each three-quarters of the way. Bake until the tops of the cupcakes spring back when pressed gently, 20 to 25 minutes. Remove the pan from the oven with oven mitts. Let the cupcakes cool 5 minutes in the pan, then remove from the pan and let cool completely on a rack.

**4** Meanwhile, make the frosting: Beat the butter, cream cheese, vanilla and salt in a large bowl with a mixer on medium speed until creamy, 1 to 2 minutes. Gradually beat in the confectioners' sugar and cocoa powder on medium-low speed until smooth, then beat on medium high until thick and fluffy, 1 to 2 more minutes.

**5** Spoon the frosting into a piping bag with a large round tip and pipe on the cupcakes (or spread the frosting on top). Sprinkle with the reserved graham cracker crumbs.

## Tip
To test for doneness, gently press the top of a cupcake with your finger. If it springs back and your finger doesn't leave a mark, the cupcakes are done!

**Did You Know?**
Enough Nutella is sold in one year to spread over more than 1,000 soccer fields!

# Chocolate-Hazelnut Cupcakes

ACTIVE: **40 min**   TOTAL: **1 hr (plus cooling)**   MAKES: **12**

## FOR THE CUPCAKES

- ¼   **cup roasted hazelnuts**
- 1   **cup all-purpose flour**
- ½   **teaspoon baking soda**
- ½   **teaspoon salt**
- ¾   **cup milk**
- ½   **cup unsweetened cocoa powder**
- 1   **cup granulated sugar**
- ¾   **cup vegetable oil**
- 1   **large egg**
- 1   **teaspoon pure vanilla extract**

## FOR THE FROSTING

- 1   **stick unsalted butter, at room temperature**
- 1   **cup confectioners' sugar**
- ½   **cup chocolate-hazelnut spread**
- 2   **tablespoons milk**
- **Chopped hazelnuts, for topping**

1. Make the cupcakes: Preheat the oven to 350˚F. Line a 12-cup muffin pan with paper liners. Finely grind the hazelnuts in a food processor. Mix the ground hazelnuts, flour, baking soda and salt in a medium bowl with a whisk.

2. Heat the milk in a small saucepan over medium heat until hot but not boiling. Put the cocoa powder in a large bowl, pour in the milk and whisk until smooth. Let cool slightly. Whisk in the granulated sugar, vegetable oil, egg and vanilla until smooth. Whisk in the flour mixture until just combined.

3. Spoon the batter into the muffin cups, filling each three-quarters of the way. Bake until the tops of the cupcakes spring back when pressed gently, 20 to 25 minutes. Remove the pan from the oven with oven mitts. Let the cupcakes cool 5 minutes in the pan, then remove from the pan and let cool completely on a rack.

4. Meanwhile, make the frosting: Combine the butter, confectioners' sugar, chocolate-hazelnut spread and milk in a large bowl. Beat with a mixer on medium speed until creamy.

5. Spoon the frosting into a piping bag with a star tip and pipe on the cupcakes (or spread the frosting on top). Sprinkle with chopped hazelnuts.

# Cookie Butter Cupcakes

ACTIVE: **40 min**   TOTAL: **1 hr (plus cooling)**   MAKES: **12**

## FOR THE CUPCAKES

- 1¼ cups all-purpose flour
- ½ teaspoon baking powder
- ½ teaspoon baking soda
- ½ teaspoon salt
- ½ teaspoon ground cinnamon
- 1 stick unsalted butter, melted
- ½ cup granulated sugar
- ½ cup packed light brown sugar
- ½ cup cookie butter (speculoos spread)
- 2 large eggs
- 1 teaspoon pure vanilla extract
- ⅓ cup mini chocolate chips

## FOR THE FROSTING

- 4 ounces semisweet chocolate, chopped
- 1 stick unsalted butter, at room temperature
- 2 cups confectioners' sugar
- 2 tablespoons unsweetened cocoa powder
- 2 tablespoons milk
- 1 teaspoon pure vanilla extract
- Chocolate sprinkles, for topping

1. Make the cupcakes: Preheat the oven to 350°F. Line a 12-cup muffin pan with paper liners. Mix the flour, baking powder, baking soda, salt and cinnamon in a medium bowl with a whisk.

2. Whisk the melted butter, granulated sugar, brown sugar, cookie butter, eggs and vanilla in a large bowl until smooth. Whisk in the flour mixture until just combined. Stir in the chocolate chips with a rubber spatula.

3. Spoon the batter into the muffin cups, filling each three-quarters of the way. Bake until the tops of the cupcakes spring back when pressed gently, 20 to 23 minutes. Remove the pan from the oven with oven mitts. Let the cupcakes cool 5 minutes in the pan, then remove from the pan and let cool completely on a rack.

4. Meanwhile, make the frosting: Put the chocolate in a microwave-safe bowl and microwave, stirring every 30 seconds, until melted. Let cool. Combine the melted chocolate, butter, confectioners' sugar, cocoa powder, milk and vanilla in a food processor. Pulse until smooth.

5. Spread the frosting on the cupcakes and top with chocolate sprinkles.

### Did You Know?

Cookie butter is made from crushed Belgian spice cookies called speculoos. America's obsession with the cookies started in the sky: In 1986, Delta started handing them out to passengers. Cookie butter came along about 25 years later!

# Mexican Hot Chocolate Cupcakes

ACTIVE: **40 min**   TOTAL: **1 hr (plus cooling)**   MAKES: **12**

## FOR THE CUPCAKES

1    **cup all-purpose flour**

¼    **cup almond flour**

1    **teaspoon ground cinnamon**

**Pinch of cayenne**

½    **teaspoon baking soda**

½    **teaspoon salt**

¾    **cup milk**

½    **cup unsweetened cocoa powder**

1    **cup granulated sugar**

¾    **cup vegetable oil**

1    **large egg**

1    **teaspoon pure vanilla extract**

## FOR THE FROSTING

4    **tablespoons unsalted butter, at room temperature**

6    **ounces cream cheese, at room temperature**

½    **cup packed light brown sugar**

1    **teaspoon pure vanilla extract**

**Pinch of salt**

1    **cup confectioners' sugar**

**Ground cinnamon and grated chocolate, for topping**

**1** Make the cupcakes: Preheat the oven to 350˚F. Line a 12-cup muffin pan with paper liners. Mix both flours, the cinnamon, cayenne, baking soda and salt with a whisk in a medium bowl.

**2** Heat the milk in a small saucepan over medium heat until hot but not boiling. Put the cocoa powder in a large bowl, pour in the hot milk and whisk until smooth. Let cool slightly. Whisk in the granulated sugar, vegetable oil, egg and vanilla until smooth. Whisk in the flour mixture until just combined.

**3** Spoon the batter into the muffin cups, filling each three-quarters of the way. Bake until the tops of the cupcakes spring back when pressed gently, 20 to 25 minutes. Remove the pan from the oven with oven mitts. Let the cupcakes cool 5 minutes in the pan, then remove from the pan and let cool completely on a rack.

**4** Meanwhile, make the frosting: Beat the butter, cream cheese, brown sugar, vanilla and salt in a large bowl with a mixer on medium speed until creamy, 1 to 2 minutes. Gradually beat in the confectioners' sugar on medium low until smooth, then beat on medium high until thick and fluffy, 1 to 2 more minutes.

**5** Spoon the frosting into a piping bag and pipe onto the cupcakes (or spread the frosting on top). Sprinkle with cinnamon and grated chocolate.

## Tip
Mexican hot chocolate is flavored with cinnamon—and sometimes a dash of chile powder. Next time you make cocoa, add a bit of each and see what you think!

**Tip**

Make sure you use white cupcake liners for these—they'll become almost transparent in the oven, so you can really see the rainbow!

# Rainbow Cupcakes

ACTIVE: 1 hr     TOTAL: 1 hr 20 min (plus cooling)     MAKES: 12

## FOR THE CUPCAKES

1¾ cups cake flour

1    teaspoon baking powder

¼    teaspoon baking soda

½    teaspoon salt

⅔    cup whole milk,
     at room temperature

Finely grated zest of 1 lemon,
     plus juice of ½ lemon

1    teaspoon pure vanilla extract

1½  sticks (12 tablespoons)
     unsalted butter,
     at room temperature

1    cup sugar

3    large egg whites,
     at room temperature

Red, orange, yellow, green, blue
     and purple gel food coloring

## FOR THE FROSTING

⅔    cup sugar

2    large egg whites,
     at room temperature

¼    cup cold water

1    teaspoon pure vanilla extract

½    teaspoon cream of tartar

Pinch of salt

**1** Make the cupcakes: Preheat the oven to 325°F. Line a 12-cup muffin pan with white paper liners. Mix the flour, baking powder, baking soda and salt in a medium bowl with a whisk. Stir the milk, lemon juice and vanilla in a small bowl using a spoon (the milk will curdle).

**2** Beat the butter, ¾ cup sugar and the lemon zest in a large bowl with a mixer on medium-high speed until light and fluffy, about 5 minutes. With the mixer on low speed, beat in the flour mixture in three batches, alternating with the milk mixture in two batches. Increase the speed to medium and beat until just combined.

**3** Beat the egg whites in a separate large bowl with a mixer on high speed until foamy. Gradually beat in the remaining ¼ cup sugar; beat until stiff glossy peaks form, about 3 minutes. Using a rubber spatula, fold the beaten egg whites into the batter in two batches.

**4** Divide the batter evenly among 6 small bowls using the rubber spatula. Tint each bowl with 1 to 3 drops gel food coloring, stirring with a separate spoon in each bowl to distribute the color.

**5** Spoon the purple batter into the muffin cups (about 1½ teaspoons per cup) and gently spread to cover the bottom; layer the blue, green, yellow, orange and red batters on top using clean spoons, gently spreading each color but making sure not to swirl the colors together. (The muffin cups will be full.) Bake until the tops of the cupcakes spring back when pressed gently, about 20 minutes. Remove the pan from the oven with oven mitts. Let the cupcakes cool 5 minutes in the pan, then remove from the pan and let cool completely on a rack.

**6** Meanwhile, make the frosting: Put the sugar, egg whites, water, vanilla, cream of tartar and salt in a large metal bowl and set over a saucepan of water (do not let the bottom of the bowl touch the water). Bring the water to a simmer under the bowl and stir the sugar mixture with a whisk until combined. With the bowl still over the simmering water, carefully beat the mixture with a hand mixer on medium-high speed until stiff glossy peaks form, 5 to 7 minutes. Remove the bowl from the saucepan with oven mitts and let cool 5 minutes. Spoon the frosting into a piping bag with a large round tip and pipe the frosting on the cupcakes.

**Did You Know?**

These cupcakes are inspired by Boston cream pie, which isn't pie at all. It's vanilla cake with a custard filling and chocolate glaze on top.

# Boston Cream Pie Cupcakes

ACTIVE: **40 min**    TOTAL: **1 hr (plus cooling)**    MAKES: **12**

## FOR THE CUPCAKES

- 1⅓ **cups all-purpose flour**
- 1 **teaspoon baking powder**
- ½ **teaspoon salt**
- 1 **stick unsalted butter, at room temperature**
- 1 **cup sugar**
- 2 **large eggs**
- 2 **teaspoons pure vanilla extract**
- ½ **cup milk**

## FOR THE GLAZE AND FILLING

- ½ **cup heavy cream**
- 4 **ounces semisweet chocolate, chopped**
- ⅔ **cup vanilla pudding**

**1** Make the cupcakes: Preheat the oven to 350°F. Line a 12-cup muffin pan with paper liners. Mix the flour, baking powder and salt in a medium bowl with a whisk.

**2** Put the butter in a large bowl and beat with a mixer on medium-high speed until smooth, about 1 minute. Add the sugar and beat until creamy, about 4 more minutes. Beat in the eggs, one at a time, then the vanilla. With the mixer on low speed, beat in the flour mixture in three batches, alternating with the milk in two batches. Increase the speed to medium high and beat until just combined.

**3** Spoon the batter into the muffin cups, filling each three-quarters of the way. Bake until the tops of the cupcakes spring back when pressed gently, 20 to 25 minutes. Remove the pan from the oven with oven mitts. Let the cupcakes cool 5 minutes in the pan, then remove from the pan and let cool completely on a rack.

**4** Meanwhile, make the glaze: Heat the heavy cream in a small saucepan over medium heat until hot. Put the chocolate in a small bowl, then carefully pour the hot cream on top and whisk until smooth. Let cool until thickened.

**5** Spoon the pudding into a piping bag with a small tip. Cut a slit into the top of each cupcake using a paring knife; pipe some pudding into each. Spoon the chocolate glaze over the cupcakes and let set.

# Lemon-Raspberry Cupcakes

ACTIVE: 40 min    TOTAL: 1 hr (plus cooling)    MAKES: 12

## FOR THE CUPCAKES

- 1⅓ cups all-purpose flour
- 1 teaspoon baking powder
- ½ teaspoon salt
- 1 stick unsalted butter, at room temperature
- 1 cup granulated sugar
- 2 large eggs
- 2 teaspoons pure vanilla extract
- ½ cup seedless raspberry jam
- 2 teaspoons grated lemon zest
- ½ cup milk

## FOR THE FROSTING

- 1½ sticks (12 tablespoons) unsalted butter, at room temperature
- 3 cups confectioners' sugar
- Pinch of salt
- 2 teaspoons pure vanilla extract
- 2 tablespoons seedless raspberry jam
- Raspberries, for topping

1. Make the cupcakes: Preheat the oven to 350°F. Line a 12-cup muffin pan with paper liners. Mix the flour, baking powder and salt in a medium bowl with a whisk.

2. Put the butter in a large bowl and beat with a mixer on medium-high speed until smooth, about 1 minute. Add the granulated sugar and beat until creamy, about 4 more minutes. Beat in the eggs, one at a time, then the vanilla, raspberry jam and lemon zest. With the mixer on low speed, beat in the flour mixture in three batches, alternating with the milk in two batches. Increase the speed to medium high and beat until just combined.

3. Spoon the batter into the muffin cups, filling each three-quarters of the way. Bake until the tops of the cupcakes spring back when pressed gently, 20 to 25 minutes. Remove the pan from the oven with oven mitts. Let the cupcakes cool 5 minutes in the pan, then remove from the pan and let cool completely on a rack.

4. Meanwhile, make the frosting: Put the butter, confectioners' sugar and salt in a large bowl and beat with a mixer on medium speed until just combined. Beat in the vanilla on medium-high speed until creamy, about 3 minutes. Add the raspberry jam and beat until fluffy, 1 more minute.

5. Spread the frosting on the cupcakes and top with raspberries.

### Tip

You can customize these cupcakes with your favorite berries— just switch up the flavor of jam and put matching berries on top!

## Did You Know?

These cupcakes taste just like peanut butter cups, a candy that H. B. Reese introduced in 1928. Reese originally worked at The Hershey Company but left and started his own candy business.

# Mini PB & Chocolate Cupcakes

ACTIVE: 1 hr    TOTAL: 1½ hr (plus cooling)    MAKES: 24

## FOR THE CUPCAKES

- 1½ sticks (12 tablespoons) unsalted butter, cut into pieces
- ½ cup unsweetened Dutch-process cocoa powder
- ¼ cup water
- 1⅓ cups packed dark brown sugar
- 1⅓ cups all-purpose flour
- ½ teaspoon baking powder
- ¼ teaspoon baking soda
- ½ teaspoon salt
- ⅓ cup buttermilk
- 1 large egg, at room temperature
- 1 teaspoon pure vanilla extract

## FOR THE TOPPING

- ½ cup heavy cream
- 1 10-ounce bag peanut butter chips

## FOR THE GLAZE

- 1 tablespoon unsalted butter
- 6 ounces milk chocolate, finely chopped
- 3 tablespoons hot water

1 Make the cupcakes: Preheat the oven to 350°F. Line a 24-cup mini-muffin pan with paper liners. Put the butter, cocoa powder and water in a microwave-safe bowl; cover with a plate or plastic wrap and microwave until the butter melts, about 2 minutes. Stir with a whisk to combine, then whisk in the brown sugar.

2 Whisk the flour, baking powder, baking soda and salt in a large bowl. Whisk in the warm cocoa mixture. In another bowl, whisk the buttermilk, egg and vanilla, then whisk into the batter until just combined.

3 Spoon the batter into the mini-muffin cups, filling each three-quarters of the way. Bake until the tops of the cupcakes spring back when pressed gently, about 20 minutes. Remove the pan from the oven with oven mitts. Let the cupcakes cool 5 minutes in the pan, then remove from the pan and let cool completely on a rack.

4 Meanwhile, make the topping: Pour the heavy cream into a small saucepan and bring to a simmer. Put the peanut butter chips in a medium bowl, then, using oven mitts, carefully pour the hot heavy cream over the chips and let stand until melted, about 5 minutes. Stir with a clean whisk until smooth. Refrigerate until the topping is set, about 10 minutes. Beat the topping with a mixer until fluffy. Spoon the topping into a piping bag with a 1-inch round tip. Pipe peaks of topping onto each cupcake. Place the cupcakes on a baking sheet and place in the freezer while you make the glaze.

5 Make the glaze: Put the butter, chocolate and hot water in a small microwave-safe bowl; cover with a plate or plastic wrap and microwave until melted, about 2 minutes. Stir with a whisk until smooth. One at a time, turn each cupcake upside down and dunk the chilled peaks into the glaze, letting the excess drip off. Return to the baking sheet. Refrigerate until the glaze is set, about 5 minutes.

# Cupcake Toppers

Pick up some candy melts at a craft store and use them to make colorful decorations.

## How to Work with Candy Melts

Put candy melts in a microwave-safe bowl and microwave at 50 percent power, stirring every 30 seconds, until smooth. Remelt as needed. Let set at room temperature or in the fridge or freezer—candy melts harden quickly!

## Varsity Letter

Draw a block letter on parchment; flip onto a baking sheet. Melt candy melts, then spoon into a resealable plastic bag and snip a corner. Using your markings as a guide, pipe an outline with candy melts. Let set slightly, then fill the letter with another color of melted candy melts. Let set.

## Tricolor Curls

Melt candy melts, then spoon into a small paper cup so it's about ¼ inch deep; freeze until set. Repeat with two more colors. Once set, tear away the paper cup to remove the candy melt block, let soften slightly and shave with a vegetable peeler to make curls.

## Flower Pop

Melt candy melts, then spoon into a resealable plastic bag and snip a corner. Pipe a flower shape on a parchment-lined baking sheet, starting from the center and working outward. Add sugar pearls or sprinkles to the center and let set. Attach a lollipop stick to the back with more melted candy melts.

## Sparkling Star

Melt candy melts, then spoon into a resealable plastic bag and snip a corner. Pipe a star shape on a parchment-lined baking sheet; sprinkle with sanding sugar and let set. Attach a lollipop stick to the back with more melted candy melts.

## Brushstrokes

Melt candy melts in three different shades. Use the back of a spoon to make small swipes of the melted candy on a parchment-lined baking sheet. Let set.

# cakes

## Tip

You can use this easy one-bowl batter to make a sheet cake instead: Just pour it into an oiled 9-by-13-inch pan and bake 40 to 45 minutes.

# Chocolate Candy Bar Layer Cake

ACTIVE: 50 min    TOTAL: 2 hr (plus cooling)    SERVES: 8 to 10

## FOR THE CAKE

½ cup vegetable oil, plus more for the pans

2 cups all-purpose flour, plus more for the pans

1¾ cups granulated sugar

¼ cup packed light brown sugar

¾ cup unsweetened cocoa powder

1½ teaspoons baking soda

1 teaspoon salt

¼ teaspoon baking powder

3 large eggs

1 cup whole milk

1 tablespoon distilled white vinegar

2 teaspoons pure vanilla extract

¼ cup hot tap water

## FOR THE FROSTING

8 ounces semisweet or milk chocolate, chopped

1 tablespoon unsweetened cocoa powder

2 teaspoons pure vanilla extract

3 sticks unsalted butter, at room temperature

½ teaspoon salt

1½ cups confectioners' sugar

½ cup finely chopped chocolate-toffee bars, plus large pieces for topping

1. Make the cake: Preheat the oven to 350°F. Brush two 9-inch round cake pans with vegetable oil. Line the bottoms with parchment paper. Brush with more oil and dust with flour, tapping out the excess. Mix the flour, granulated sugar, brown sugar, cocoa powder, baking soda, salt and baking powder in a large bowl with a mixer on low speed until combined. Add the eggs, milk, vegetable oil, vinegar and vanilla. Increase the speed to medium and beat until smooth, about 2 minutes. Beat in the hot water until smooth.

2. Scrape the batter into the pans using a rubber spatula. Tap the bottoms of the pans against the counter to remove any air bubbles. Bake until a toothpick inserted into the center of the cakes comes out clean, 40 to 45 minutes. Remove the pans from the oven with oven mitts. Put the pans on a rack and let cool 10 minutes. Loosen the edges of the cakes with a small knife, remove the cakes from the pans and let cool completely on the rack. Remove the parchment.

3. Meanwhile, make the frosting: Put the chocolate in a microwave-safe bowl and microwave 30 seconds at a time, stirring, until melted. Let cool slightly. Stir together the cocoa powder and vanilla in a small bowl. Beat the butter and salt in a large bowl with a mixer on medium speed until fluffy and smooth, 1 to 2 minutes. Add the melted chocolate and beat until combined. Gradually add the confectioners' sugar and beat until smooth. Add the cocoa mixture. Increase the speed to medium high and beat until smooth and fluffy, 1 to 2 minutes.

4. Put 1 cake layer on a cake stand or serving plate and spread with 1 heaping cup frosting using an offset spatula. Sprinkle with the finely chopped candy and top with the other cake layer. Spread the remaining frosting on the top and sides of the cake. Refrigerate until set, about 30 minutes. Top with large pieces of candy.

## Did You Know?

Heath Bars were invented in 1928 by two brothers, Bayard and Everett Heath. Their father owned a dairy facility, and local customers could get Heath Bars delivered with their milk!

# Basic Vanilla Cake

ACTIVE: 50 min    TOTAL: 1 hr 20 min (plus cooling)    SERVES: 8 to 10

## FOR THE CAKE

- **2** sticks unsalted butter, at room temperature, plus more for the pans
- **3** cups all-purpose flour, plus more for the pans
- **1** tablespoon baking powder
- **½** teaspoon salt
- **1¼** cups granulated sugar
- **4** large eggs, at room temperature
- **1** tablespoon pure vanilla extract
- **1¼** cups whole milk

## FOR THE FROSTING

- **2** sticks unsalted butter, at room temperature
- **Pinch of salt**
- **3** cups confectioners' sugar
- **1** tablespoon vanilla extract
- **1 to 2** tablespoons whole milk
- **Sprinkles, for decorating**

1. Make the cake: Preheat the oven to 350°F. Butter two 9-inch round cake pans and line the bottoms with parchment paper; butter the parchment. Dust the pans with flour, tapping out the excess. Combine the flour, baking powder and salt in a medium bowl with a whisk.

2. Beat the butter and granulated sugar in a large bowl with a mixer on medium-high speed until light and fluffy, about 3 minutes. Reduce the mixer speed to medium; beat in the eggs, one at a time, scraping down the bowl with a rubber spatula as needed. Beat in the vanilla. Beat in the flour mixture in three batches, alternating with the milk in two batches, until just smooth.

3. Scrape the batter into the pans using the rubber spatula. Bake until the cakes are lightly golden on top and a toothpick inserted into the center comes out clean, 30 to 35 minutes. Remove the pans from the oven with oven mitts. Put the pans on a rack and let cool 10 minutes. Loosen the edges of the cakes with a small knife, remove the cakes from the pans and let cool completely on the rack. Remove the parchment.

4. Meanwhile, make the frosting: Beat the butter and salt in a large bowl with a mixer on medium speed until smooth and fluffy, 1 to 2 minutes. Gradually beat in the confectioners' sugar until smooth. Add the vanilla, increase the mixer speed to medium high and beat until thick, about 2 more minutes. Add the milk a little at a time and beat until the frosting is spreadable but not runny.

5. Put 1 cake layer on a platter. Spread 1 cup frosting on top with an offset spatula. Top with the other cake layer. Spread the remaining frosting on the top and sides of the cake. Decorate with sprinkles.

## Did You Know?

A classic Oreo cookie is 29% cream and 71% cookie. Which part is your favorite?

# Cookies-and-Cream Cake

ACTIVE: 50 min    TOTAL: 1 hr 20 min (plus cooling)    SERVES: 8 to 10

## FOR THE CAKE

- **2 sticks unsalted butter,** at room temperature, plus more for the pans
- **3 cups all-purpose flour,** plus more for the pans
- **1 tablespoon baking powder**
- **½ teaspoon salt**
- **1¼ cups granulated sugar**
- **4 large eggs,** at room temperature
- **1 tablespoon pure** vanilla extract
- **1¼ cups whole milk**

## FOR THE FROSTING

- **6 ounces white chocolate,** finely chopped
- **3 sticks unsalted butter,** at room temperature
- **1 teaspoon pure** vanilla extract
- **Pinch of salt**
- **3 cups confectioners' sugar**
- **15 chocolate sandwich** cookies, chopped

1. Make the cake: Preheat the oven to 350°F. Butter two 9-inch round cake pans and line the bottoms with parchment paper; butter the parchment. Dust the pans with flour, tapping out the excess. Combine the flour, baking powder and salt in a bowl with a whisk.

2. Beat the butter and granulated sugar in a large bowl with a mixer on medium-high speed until light and fluffy, about 3 minutes. Reduce the mixer speed to medium; beat in the eggs, one at a time, scraping down the bowl with a rubber spatula as needed. Beat in the vanilla. Beat in the flour mixture in three batches, alternating with the milk in two batches, until just smooth.

3. Scrape the batter into the pans using the rubber spatula. Bake until the cakes are lightly golden on top and a toothpick inserted into the center comes out clean, 30 to 35 minutes. Remove the pans from the oven with oven mitts. Put the pans on a rack and let cool 10 minutes. Loosen the edges of the cakes with a small knife, remove the cakes from the pans and let cool completely on the rack. Remove the parchment.

4. Meanwhile, make the frosting: Put the white chocolate in a microwave-safe bowl and microwave 30 seconds at a time, stirring, until smooth; let cool slightly. Beat the butter, vanilla and salt in a large bowl with a mixer on medium-high speed until smooth, about 1 minute. Add the melted white chocolate and beat until combined. Gradually beat in the confectioners' sugar until smooth.

5. Place 1 cake layer on a platter. Spread 1 cup frosting on top with an offset spatula. Sprinkle with ½ cup chopped cookies. Top with the other cake layer. Spread the remaining frosting on the top and sides of the cake. Press the remaining cookies into the sides.

## Tip

To cut a cake into thinner layers, mark around the sides of the cake with toothpicks so you know where to cut. Then use a long serrated knife to slice it.

# Strawberry Shortcake Layer Cake

ACTIVE: 50 min    TOTAL: 1 hr 40 min (plus cooling)    SERVES: 8

## FOR THE CAKE

- **5** tablespoons unsalted butter, melted, plus more for the pan
- **1⅓** cups all-purpose flour, plus more for the pan
- **1¼** cups granulated sugar
- **1¼** teaspoons baking powder
- **½** teaspoon salt
- **1½** teaspoons vanilla bean paste (or seeds from ½ vanilla bean)
- **2** large eggs, at room temperature, lightly beaten
- **¾** cup whole milk, at room temperature
- **½** teaspoon finely grated lemon zest

## FOR THE TOPPINGS AND FILLING

- **1½** quarts strawberries, hulled
- **1** tablespoon water
- **1** tablespoon strawberry jelly
- **3** tablespoons confectioners' sugar
- **1** tablespoon fresh lemon juice
- **1½** cups cold heavy cream
- **¼** teaspoon pure vanilla extract

1. Make the cake: Preheat the oven to 350˚F. Butter an 8-inch round cake pan, then line the bottom with parchment paper; butter the parchment. Dust the pan with flour, tapping out the excess.

2. Combine the flour, granulated sugar, baking powder and salt in a large bowl with a whisk. Whisk the melted butter, vanilla bean paste, beaten eggs, milk and lemon zest in a medium bowl until just smooth. Add the egg mixture to the flour mixture and stir with a wooden spoon to combine.

3. Scrape the batter into the pan using a rubber spatula. Bake until a toothpick inserted into the center of the cake comes out clean, 35 to 40 minutes. Remove the pan from the oven with oven mitts. Put the pan on a rack and let cool 10 minutes. Loosen the edges of the cake with a small knife, remove the cake from the pan and let cool completely on the rack. Remove the parchment.

4. Meanwhile, make the toppings and filling: Halve 16 strawberries. Whisk the water and strawberry jelly in a medium bowl until smooth. Add the halved strawberries and toss to coat; set aside. Thinly slice the remaining strawberries with a paring knife. Toss with 2 tablespoons confectioners' sugar and the lemon juice in another medium bowl; set aside. In a large bowl, beat the heavy cream, the remaining 1 tablespoon confectioners' sugar and the vanilla extract with a mixer on medium-high speed until soft peaks form. Refrigerate the whipped cream until ready to assemble.

5. Carefully slice the cake in half horizontally with a long serrated knife. Place the bottom half cut-side up on a platter. Drizzle the juices from the thinly sliced berries over the cut sides of both cake halves. Using a rubber spatula, stir a few tablespoons of the whipped cream into the sliced berries, then spoon them over the bottom cake layer. Cover with the other cake layer, then top with the remaining whipped cream. Top with the halved strawberries and their juices.

# Triple Chocolate Cake

ACTIVE: 1 hr   TOTAL: 2 hr 50 min (plus cooling)   SERVES: 8 to 10

## FOR THE CAKE

- 1 stick unsalted butter, at room temperature, plus more for the pans
- 2½ cups all-purpose flour, plus more for the pans
- 4 ounces semisweet chocolate, chopped
- 1½ cups whole milk
- ½ cup water
- ½ cup unsweetened cocoa powder
- 1½ teaspoons baking powder
- 1 teaspoon baking soda
- ½ teaspoon salt
- ½ cup vegetable oil
- 1½ cups packed dark brown sugar
- ½ cup granulated sugar
- 1 tablespoon pure vanilla extract
- 4 large eggs

## FOR THE FROSTING

- 24 ounces semisweet chocolate, chopped
- ⅓ cup light corn syrup
- ½ cup hot water
- 1 tablespoon pure vanilla extract
- 2½ sticks unsalted butter, cut into pieces, at room temperature
- 2½ cups confectioners' sugar

1. Make the cake: Preheat the oven to 350°F. Butter two 8-inch round cake pans and dust with flour, tapping out the excess. Combine the chocolate, milk and water in a microwave-safe bowl. Microwave 30 seconds at a time, stirring, until the chocolate is melted. Whisk until smooth, then let cool. Sift the flour, cocoa powder, baking powder, baking soda and salt through a sieve into a medium bowl.

2. Beat the butter in a large bowl with a mixer on medium speed until creamy, about 4 minutes. Add the vegetable oil, brown sugar, granulated sugar and vanilla; beat until fluffy, about 4 more minutes. Add the eggs, one at a time, beating until combined. Reduce the mixer speed to low and add the flour mixture in three batches, alternating with the melted chocolate mixture in two batches; beat until just combined.

3. Scrape the batter into the pans using a rubber spatula and smooth the tops. Bake until a toothpick inserted into the center comes out clean, 45 to 50 minutes. Remove the pans from the oven with oven mitts. Put the pans on a rack and let cool 20 minutes. Loosen the edges of the cakes with a small knife, remove the cakes from the pans and let cool completely on the rack.

4. Preheat the oven to 350°F again. Line a rimmed baking sheet with foil. Carefully cut each cake in half horizontally with a long serrated knife; you will have 4 thinner layers. Crumble 1 layer into small pieces on the baking sheet. Bake until dry, about 20 minutes. Remove the pan from the oven with oven mitts. Let cool completely. Cover the small cake pieces with parchment paper and crush with the bottom of a saucepan to make coarse crumbs.

5. Make the frosting: Combine the chocolate, corn syrup and hot water in a large heatproof bowl. Set the bowl over a pot filled with a few inches of simmering water (do not let the bottom of the bowl touch the water); stir the chocolate mixture until melted, about 5 minutes. Carefully remove the bowl from the pot with oven mitts and let cool 10 minutes. Add the vanilla to the bowl and beat with a mixer on high speed, then beat in the butter, 1 piece at a time, until fluffy. Gradually add the confectioners' sugar and beat until creamy. Refrigerate, stirring occasionally, until thick enough to spread, about 10 minutes.

6. Put 1 cake layer on a platter. Spread 1 heaping cup frosting on top with an offset spatula. Top with another cake layer, spread with more frosting and add the last cake layer. Cover the top and sides with the remaining frosting. Press the cake crumbs all over the cake.

**Tip**

Melting chocolate can be tricky—it clumps when it gets too hot. To prevent this, melt it for 30 seconds at a time in the microwave, or in a heatproof bowl set over a pan of simmering water.

**Tip**

Assemble this cake close to dessert time—the marshmallow cream will start to ooze the longer it sits. Don't worry if it's a little drippy though: That's the idea!

# S'mores Cake

ACTIVE: 1 hr    TOTAL: 3 hr (plus cooling)    SERVES: 8 to 10

## FOR THE CAKE

Cooking spray

1 cup unsweetened cocoa powder

1½ cups boiling water

2½ cups all-purpose flour

2 cups sugar

1½ teaspoons baking powder

1 teaspoon baking soda

1 teaspoon salt

3 large eggs, at room temperature

¾ cup vegetable oil

½ cup sour cream

2 teaspoons pure vanilla extract

## FOR THE GANACHE

½ cup heavy cream

4 ounces semisweet chocolate, finely chopped

Pinch of salt

½ teaspoon pure vanilla extract

## FOR THE FILLING

8 whole graham crackers, crushed

2 tablespoons unsalted butter, melted

Pinch of salt

Vegetable oil, for the spatula

1 16-ounce container marshmallow cream

1. Make the cake: Preheat the oven to 350˚F. Coat two 9-inch round cake pans with cooking spray and line the bottoms with parchment paper. Carefully mix the cocoa powder and boiling water in a medium bowl with a whisk.

2. Combine the flour, sugar, baking powder, baking soda and salt in a large bowl with the whisk. Add the eggs, vegetable oil, sour cream and vanilla and beat with a mixer on medium speed until smooth, about 1 minute. Beat in the cocoa mixture on low speed in a steady stream until just combined. Finish mixing with a rubber spatula.

3. Scrape the batter into the pans using the rubber spatula. Tap the bottoms of the pans against the counter to help the batter settle. Bake until a toothpick inserted into the center of the cakes comes out clean, 30 to 40 minutes. Remove the pans from the oven with oven mitts. Put the pans on a rack and let cool 10 minutes. Loosen the edges of the cakes with a small knife, remove the cakes from the pans and let cool completely on the rack. Remove the parchment.

4. Meanwhile, make the ganache: Combine the heavy cream, chocolate and salt in a heatproof bowl. Set the bowl over a saucepan filled with a few inches of simmering water (do not let the bottom of the bowl touch the water); stir the chocolate mixture until melted and smooth. Stir in the vanilla. Carefully remove the bowl from the pan with oven mitts and set aside at room temperature until the ganache is cool and thick but still pourable, about 1 hour.

5. While the ganache cools, make the filling: Preheat the oven to 350˚F again. Toss the graham cracker crumbs, melted butter and salt in a bowl. Spread out on a baking sheet. Bake, stirring occasionally, until toasted, 8 to 10 minutes. Remove the pan from the oven with oven mitts. Let cool.

6. Carefully slice each cake in half horizontally with a long serrated knife; you will have 4 thinner layers. Place 1 cake layer on a platter. Using an oiled offset spatula, spread one-third of the marshmallow cream on top, stopping about 1 inch from the edge (microwave the marshmallow cream for 15 seconds to soften, if needed). Sprinkle one-third of the graham cracker crumbs on top. Repeat the layering (cake, marshmallow, crumbs) two more times, then top with the final cake layer. Save a few tablespoons of the crumbs for topping.

7. Pour the ganache over the cake, letting it drip down the sides. Top with the reserved graham cracker crumbs.

# ⇒ Rainbow ⇐
# Layer Cake

Pick your favorite colors, then create your ultimate layer cake!

## Tip

The easiest-ever cake-decorating trick: Cover the whole thing with nonpareils! Start with a thin layer of frosting, then set the cake on a cake plate in the sink so you don't end up with nonpareils all over the floor. You'll need about ¾ cup nonpareils for a 9-inch layer cake.

## Make the Batter

• Preheat the oven to 350°F. Butter four 9-inch round cake pans and line the bottoms with parchment paper. Combine 2¼ cups granulated sugar and 1 cup vegetable oil in a large bowl and beat with a mixer on medium-high speed until creamy, 3 minutes. Beat in 4 eggs, one at a time. Add 2 teaspoons vanilla and beat on high speed until fluffy, about 2 minutes.

• Mix 3¾ cups all-purpose flour, ¾ teaspoon baking soda and ½ teaspoon salt in a medium bowl with a whisk. With the mixer on low speed, beat the flour mixture into the sugar mixture in three batches, alternating with 1½ cups buttermilk total in two batches; beat until combined.

## Pick Your Colors

For extra bright colors, use gel food coloring (versus liquid).
It's super concentrated, so you don't need to add as much.

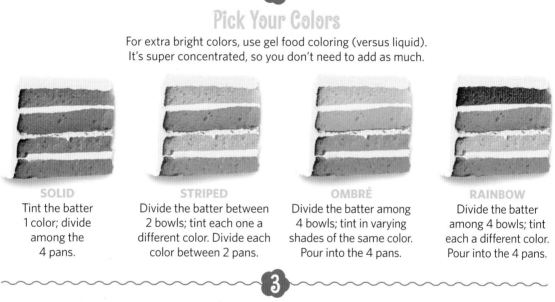

**SOLID**
Tint the batter 1 color; divide among the 4 pans.

**STRIPED**
Divide the batter between 2 bowls; tint each one a different color. Divide each color between 2 pans.

**OMBRÉ**
Divide the batter among 4 bowls; tint in varying shades of the same color. Pour into the 4 pans.

**RAINBOW**
Divide the batter among 4 bowls; tint each a different color. Pour into the 4 pans.

## Bake the Cakes

Bake 2 pans at a time until a toothpick inserted into the center of the cakes comes out clean, about 15 minutes. Remove the pans from the oven with oven mitts. Put the pans on a rack and let the cakes cool 15 minutes, then remove the cakes to the rack to cool completely. Remove the parchment.

## Make the Frosting

• Beat 8 sticks unsalted butter (cut into pieces and at room temperature) and a pinch of salt in a large bowl with a mixer on medium speed until fluffy, 2 minutes. Gradually beat in 10 cups confectioners' sugar until smooth. Add 2 tablespoons vanilla. Increase the speed to medium high and beat until thick, 2 minutes. Gradually beat in 6 to 8 tablespoons milk until spreadable.

• Stack the cake layers on a cake stand or platter, spreading about 1½ cups frosting between the layers using an offset spatula. Cover the whole cake with the remaining frosting.

# Red Velvet Layer Cake

ACTIVE: 1 hr    TOTAL: 2 hr (plus cooling)    SERVES: 8 to 10

## FOR THE CAKE

- 12 tablespoons (1½ sticks) unsalted butter, at room temperature, plus more for the pans
- 3 cups cake flour (sift it through a sieve before measuring)
- 3 tablespoons unsweetened Dutch-process cocoa powder
- 1 teaspoon baking soda
- ½ teaspoon salt
- 1¾ cups granulated sugar
- ⅓ cup vegetable oil
- 3 large eggs, at room temperature
- 1 tablespoon red liquid food coloring
- 2 teaspoons apple cider vinegar
- 1 teaspoon pure vanilla extract
- 1 cup buttermilk

## FOR THE FROSTING

- 4 8-ounce packages cream cheese, at room temperature
- 2 sticks unsalted butter, at room temperature
- 2 pounds (about 8 cups) confectioners' sugar
- 1 tablespoon fresh lemon juice
- ½ teaspoon pure vanilla extract
- ⅛ teaspoon salt

1. Make the cake: Preheat the oven to 350˚F. Butter two 9-inch round cake pans and line the bottoms with parchment paper; butter the parchment. Combine the flour, cocoa powder, baking soda and salt in a medium bowl with a whisk.

2. Beat the granulated sugar, butter and vegetable oil in a large bowl with a mixer on medium-high speed until fluffy, about 4 minutes. Beat in the eggs, one at a time. Beat in the food coloring, vinegar and vanilla. Reduce the mixer speed to low; add the flour mixture in three batches, alternating with the buttermilk in two batches; beat until just combined.

3. Scrape the batter into the pans using a rubber spatula. Bake until a toothpick inserted into the center of the cakes comes out clean, 35 to 40 minutes. Remove the pans from the oven with oven mitts. Put the pans on a rack and let cool 10 minutes. Loosen the edges of the cakes with a small knife, remove the cakes from the pans and let cool completely on the rack. Remove the parchment.

4. Carefully slice the cakes in half horizontally with a long serrated knife; you will have 4 thinner layers.

5. Make the frosting: Beat the cream cheese and butter in a large bowl with a mixer on medium-high speed until fluffy. Add the confectioners' sugar, lemon juice, vanilla and salt; beat until smooth.

6. Put 1 cake layer on a platter; spread 1¼ cups frosting on top with an offset spatula. Repeat to make 4 layers, ending with a cake layer. Cover the whole cake with a thin coating of frosting. Refrigerate the cake 15 minutes. Cover with the remaining frosting.

# Root Beer Bundt Cake

ACTIVE: 45 min    TOTAL: 1 hr 40 min (plus cooling)    SERVES: 8 to 10

## FOR THE CAKE

- **1**   **stick unsalted butter, plus more for the pan**
- **2**   **cups all-purpose flour, plus more for dusting**
- **2¼ cups root beer**
- **1**   **cup unsweetened cocoa powder**
- **2**   **ounces bittersweet chocolate, chopped**
- **1**   **cup granulated sugar**
- **½**   **cup packed dark brown sugar**
- **1¼ teaspoons baking soda**
- **½**   **teaspoon ground allspice**
- **1**   **teaspoon salt**
- **3**   **large eggs, lightly beaten**

## FOR THE GLAZE

- **¼**   **cup root beer**
- **Pinch of salt**
- **2½ cups confectioners' sugar**
- **1**   **teaspoon pure vanilla extract**

1. Make the cake: Preheat the oven to 325°F. Butter a 12-cup bundt pan and dust with flour, tapping out the excess. Heat 2 cups root beer, the cocoa powder, chocolate and butter in a large saucepan over medium heat until the butter melts. Add the granulated and brown sugars and stir with a whisk until dissolved. Remove from the heat and let cool.

2. Combine the flour, baking soda, allspice and salt in a medium bowl with a whisk. Whisk the beaten eggs into the saucepan with the root beer mixture. Gently stir in the flour mixture with a rubber spatula (the batter will be slightly lumpy).

3. Scrape the batter into the bundt pan using the rubber spatula. Bake, rotating the pan with oven mitts halfway through, until a toothpick inserted into the center of the cake comes out clean, 55 minutes to 1 hour. Remove the pan from the oven with oven mitts. Put the pan on a rack, then gently poke the warm cake all over with a skewer. Pour the remaining ¼ cup root beer over the cake; let cool in the pan, 20 minutes. Turn out the cake onto a serving plate and let cool completely.

4. Meanwhile, make the glaze: Whisk the root beer, salt, confectioners' sugar and vanilla in a bowl until smooth. Pour the glaze over the cake.

### Did You Know?

The original Tunnel of Fudge Cake was created by Ella Rita Helfrich, a home baker from Houston who entered her recipe in the 1966 Pillsbury Bake-Off. She didn't win (she got second place!), but her cake is still one of Pillsbury's most requested recipes.

# Peanut Tunnel of Fudge Cake

ACTIVE: 45 min    TOTAL: 1 hr 45 min (plus cooling)    SERVES: 8 to 10

## FOR THE CAKE

Cooking spray

2¼ cups all-purpose flour

2 cups honey-roasted peanuts

4 large eggs plus 2 egg yolks

2½ sticks unsalted butter,
    cut into pieces,
    at room temperature

1½ cups granulated sugar

¾ cup packed dark brown sugar

⅓ cup roasted peanut oil

1 teaspoon pure vanilla extract

½ teaspoon kosher salt

1½ cups confectioners' sugar

¾ cup unsweetened
    cocoa powder

## FOR THE GLAZE

1½ cups confectioners' sugar

3 tablespoons milk

¼ cup creamy peanut butter

1 teaspoon pure vanilla extract

¼ teaspoon kosher salt

1. Make the cake: Position a rack in the lower third of the oven; preheat to 350°F. Generously coat a 10- to 15-cup bundt pan with cooking spray. Combine the flour and peanuts in a large bowl. Lightly stir the whole eggs and egg yolks with a fork in a small bowl until they are just streaky.

2. Beat the butter in a large bowl with a mixer on medium speed until fluffy, about 2 minutes. Add the granulated sugar, then the brown sugar and beat until fluffy, about 4 minutes. Beat in the peanut oil, vanilla and salt; scrape down the bowl. Reduce the mixer speed to low and add the beaten eggs in three additions. Beat in the confectioners' sugar and cocoa powder until just combined; do not overmix. Fold in the flour-peanut mixture with a rubber spatula.

3. Scrape the batter into the bundt pan using the rubber spatula and spread it evenly. Bake 45 minutes (be careful not to overbake). Remove the pan from the oven with oven mitts. Put the pan on a rack and let cool 20 minutes. Gently press down on the cake to remove any air bubbles in the tunnel (it's OK if the cake cracks a little bit), then let cool completely in the pan.

4. Make the glaze: Mix the confectioners' sugar, milk, peanut butter, vanilla and salt in a medium bowl with a whisk until smooth. Turn out the cake onto a platter and pour the glaze on top.

## Tip

Be careful not to overbake this cake. You want the "tunnel of fudge" to stay nice and gooey!

# Mint Chip Sheet Cake

ACTIVE: 40 min   TOTAL: 2 hr (plus cooling)   SERVES: 10 to 12

## FOR THE CAKE

Unsalted butter, for the pan

¾   cup unsweetened Dutch-process cocoa powder, plus more for the pan

2¼ cups all-purpose flour

1¼ teaspoons baking soda

¾   teaspoon salt

½   teaspoon baking powder

1   cup boiling water

2   cups granulated sugar

½   cup vegetable oil

½   cup buttermilk

2   large eggs, at room temperature

1   tablespoon pure vanilla extract

## FOR THE FROSTING

3   sticks unsalted butter, at room temperature

Pinch of salt

4   cups confectioners' sugar

1   teaspoon pure vanilla extract

1   teaspoon peppermint extract

2   tablespoons whole milk

2 to 3 drops green liquid food coloring

½   cup mini chocolate chips, plus more for topping

1. Make the cake: Preheat the oven to 350°F. Butter a 9-by-13-inch baking pan and dust with cocoa powder, tapping out the excess. Combine the flour, baking soda, salt and baking powder in a large bowl with a whisk.

2. Carefully pour the boiling water over the cocoa powder in another large bowl; whisk until smooth. Let cool 10 minutes. Whisk in the granulated sugar, vegetable oil, buttermilk, eggs and vanilla. Whisk in the flour mixture in two batches until smooth.

3. Scrape the batter into the pan using a rubber spatula. Tap the bottom of the pan against the counter to release any air bubbles. Bake until a toothpick inserted into the center of the cake comes out clean, 35 to 45 minutes. Remove the pan from the oven with oven mitts. Put the pan on a rack and let the cake cool completely.

4. Meanwhile, make the frosting: Beat the butter and salt in a large bowl with a mixer on medium-high speed until fluffy, about 2 minutes. Gradually beat in the confectioners' sugar on low speed until combined. Beat in the vanilla and peppermint extracts on medium-high speed until fluffy, about 3 minutes. Beat in the milk until combined, 1 to 2 more minutes. Beat in the food coloring, then stir in the chocolate chips with a rubber spatula.

5. Spread the frosting on the cake using an offset spatula. Sprinkle with more chocolate chips. Refrigerate 30 minutes before serving.

## Tip

You can make an extra-large, thin sheet cake using any of the recipes on pages 146 to 149. Just pour the batter into a buttered 13-by-18-inch rimmed baking sheet and bake 30 to 35 minutes.

# Lemon Sheet Cake

ACTIVE: 50 min    TOTAL: 1 hr 45 min (plus cooling)    SERVES: 10 to 12

## FOR THE CAKE

1½ sticks (12 tablespoons) unsalted butter, at room temperature, plus more for the pan

3 cups all-purpose flour, plus more for the pan

1½ teaspoons baking powder

1 teaspoon salt

¼ teaspoon baking soda

¼ cup vegetable oil

1½ cups granulated sugar

2 tablespoons grated lemon zest, plus 2 tablespoons lemon juice

3 large eggs, at room temperature

1 tablespoon pure vanilla extract

1¼ cups buttermilk

## FOR THE FROSTING

3 sticks unsalted butter, at room temperature

1 tablespoon grated lemon zest, plus 2 tablespoons lemon juice

Pinch of salt

4 cups confectioners' sugar

2 tablespoons whole milk

2 to 3 drops yellow liquid food coloring

Yellow sanding sugar, for topping

1. Make the cake: Preheat the oven to 350˚F. Butter a 9-by-13-inch baking pan and dust with flour, tapping out the excess. Combine the flour, baking powder, salt and baking soda in a medium bowl with a whisk.

2. Beat the butter and vegetable oil in a large bowl with a mixer on medium-high speed until combined. Add the granulated sugar, lemon zest and lemon juice and beat until fluffy, about 4 minutes. Beat in the eggs, one at a time, then the vanilla. Reduce the speed to low and beat in the flour mixture in three batches, alternating with the buttermilk in two batches. Beat on medium-high speed until combined.

3. Scrape the batter into the pan using a rubber spatula. Tap the bottom of the pan against the counter to release any air bubbles. Bake until a toothpick inserted into the center of the cake comes out clean, 35 to 40 minutes. Remove the pan from the oven with oven mitts. Put the pan on a rack and let the cake cool completely.

4. Meanwhile, make the frosting: Beat the butter, lemon zest and salt in a large bowl with a mixer on medium-high speed until fluffy, about 2 minutes. Gradually beat in the confectioners' sugar on low speed until combined. Add the lemon juice and beat on medium-high speed until fluffy, about 3 minutes. Beat in the milk until combined, 1 to 2 more minutes. Beat in the food coloring.

5. Spread the frosting on the cake using an offset spatula. Sprinkle with yellow sanding sugar. Refrigerate 30 minutes before serving.

# PB&J Sheet Cake

## FOR THE CAKE

- 1½ sticks (12 tablespoons) unsalted butter, at room temperature, plus more for the pan
- 3 cups all-purpose flour, plus more for the pan
- 1½ teaspoons baking powder
- 1 teaspoon salt
- ¼ teaspoon baking soda
- ¼ cup vegetable oil
- 1½ cups granulated sugar
- 3 large eggs, at room temperature
- 1 tablespoon pure vanilla extract
- 1¼ cups buttermilk
- ½ cup grape jelly

## FOR THE FROSTING

- 1½ sticks (12 tablespoons) unsalted butter, at room temperature
- 1 cup creamy peanut butter
- 1½ cups confectioners' sugar
- Chopped salted peanuts, for topping

1. Make the cake: Preheat the oven to 350˚F. Butter a 9-by-13-inch baking pan and dust with flour, tapping out the excess. Combine the flour, baking powder, salt and baking soda in a medium bowl with a whisk.

2. Beat the butter and vegetable oil in a large bowl with a mixer on medium-high speed until combined. Add the granulated sugar and beat until fluffy, about 4 minutes. Beat in the eggs, one at a time, then the vanilla. Reduce the speed to low and beat in the flour mixture in three batches, alternating with the buttermilk in two batches. Beat on medium-high speed until well combined.

3. Scrape the batter into the pan with a rubber spatula. Tap the bottom of the pan against the counter to release any air bubbles. Bake until a toothpick inserted into the center of the cake comes out clean, 35 to 40 minutes. Remove the pan from the oven with oven mitts. Put the pan on a rack and let the cake cool completely.

4. Poke holes ½ inch apart in the cooled cake using a straw. Spread the jelly over the top with an offset spatula, gently pressing it into the holes.

5. Make the frosting: Beat the butter and peanut butter in a large bowl with a mixer on medium-high speed until fluffy, about 2 minutes. Beat in the confectioners' sugar on low speed, then beat on medium high until fluffy again, about 2 more minutes.

6. Spread the frosting on the cake using an offset spatula. Refrigerate 30 minutes before serving. Top with peanuts.

## Did You Know?

If you don't have buttermilk, fake it! Use 1¼ cups whole milk but replace 1 tablespoon of the milk with 1 tablespoon white vinegar or lemon juice. Stir, then let stand for 5 minutes before using. (It will curdle a bit.)

# Rainbow Sheet Cake

ACTIVE: 50 min    TOTAL: 2 hr (plus cooling)    SERVES: 10 to 12

## FOR THE CAKE

1½ sticks (12 tablespoons) unsalted butter, at room temperature, plus more for the pan

3 cups all-purpose flour, plus more for the pan

1½ teaspoons baking powder

1 teaspoon salt

¼ teaspoon baking soda

¼ cup vegetable oil

1½ cups granulated sugar

3 large eggs, at room temperature

1 tablespoon pure vanilla extract

1¼ cups buttermilk

1 to 2 drops each of yellow, red, purple and green gel food coloring

## FOR THE FROSTING

3 sticks unsalted butter, at room temperature

Pinch of salt

4 cups confectioners' sugar

1 tablespoon pure vanilla extract

2 tablespoons whole milk

Rainbow nonpareils, for topping

1. Make the cake: Preheat the oven to 350°F. Butter a 9-by-13-inch baking pan and dust with flour, tapping out the excess. Combine the flour, baking powder, salt and baking soda in a medium bowl with a whisk.

2. Beat the butter and vegetable oil in a large bowl with a mixer on medium-high speed until combined. Add the granulated sugar and beat until fluffy, about 4 minutes. Beat in the eggs, one at a time, then the vanilla. Reduce the speed to low and beat in the flour mixture in three batches, alternating with the buttermilk in two batches. Beat on medium-high speed until well combined.

3. Divide the batter among 4 small bowls. Add a different color food coloring to each bowl and stir until the color is evenly mixed in.

4. Dollop the batter into the pan by spoonfuls, alternating colors. Lightly swirl with a knife or rubber spatula. Tap the bottom of the pan against the counter to release any air bubbles. Bake until a toothpick inserted into the center of the cake comes out clean, 35 to 40 minutes. Remove the pan from the oven with oven mitts. Put the pan on a rack and let the cake cool completely.

5. Meanwhile, make the frosting: Beat the butter and salt in a large bowl with a mixer on medium-high speed until fluffy, about 2 minutes. Gradually beat in the confectioners' sugar on low speed until combined. Beat in the vanilla on medium-high speed until fluffy, about 3 minutes. Beat in the milk until combined, 1 to 2 more minutes.

6. Spread the frosting on the cake using an offset spatula. Sprinkle with rainbow nonpareils. Refrigerate 30 minutes before serving.

## Tip

You can make this cake with any color combo: Use four shades of your favorite color, or swap out the primary colors here for unicorn ones: pink, purple and teal!

# Tres Leches Cake with Mango

ACTIVE: 50 min    TOTAL: 2 hr 10 min    SERVES: 8 to 10

## FOR THE CAKE

Vegetable oil, for the pan

4    large eggs

1    cup sugar

⅔    cup unsalted butter, melted

1    teaspoon pure vanilla extract

2¼ cups whole milk

1½ cups cake flour

1    teaspoon baking powder

¼    teaspoon salt

1    12-ounce can evaporated milk

1    14-ounce can sweetened condensed milk

## FOR THE TOPPING

3    cups chopped fresh mangoes

3    tablespoons sugar

1    cup heavy cream

Ground cinnamon, for topping

1. Make the cake: Preheat the oven to 350˚F. Coat an 8-inch square baking pan with vegetable oil and line the bottom with parchment paper. Beat the eggs and sugar in a large bowl with a mixer until pale and slightly thick, about 6 minutes. Slowly beat in the melted butter, then beat in the vanilla and ¼ cup whole milk.

2. Combine the flour, baking powder and salt in a medium bowl with a whisk. Using a sieve, sift the flour mixture over the egg mixture, then gently fold everything together with a rubber spatula to make a thick batter.

3. Scrape the batter into the pan using the rubber spatula. Bake until a toothpick inserted into the center of the cake comes out clean, about 30 minutes. Remove the pan from the oven with oven mitts. Loosen the edges of the cake with a small knife but leave the cake in the pan.

4. Whisk the remaining 2 cups whole milk, the evaporated milk and the condensed milk in a bowl. Pierce the warm cake all over with a fork, then pour the milk mixture evenly on top. Cover and refrigerate at least 1 hour or overnight.

5. Before serving, make the topping: Puree half the mangoes in a blender with 2 tablespoons sugar. Pour into a bowl and stir in the remaining mangoes. In a separate bowl, beat the heavy cream and remaining 1 tablespoon sugar with a mixer until soft peaks form. Slice the cake into squares; top each piece with whipped cream and sprinkle with cinnamon. Serve the mango topping on the side.

### Did You Know?

This cake is soaked in three different kinds of milk (tres leches means "three milks" in Spanish). It's extra rich and delicious!

MILK
EVAPORATED milk
SWEETENED condensed milk